Palgrave Studies in Economic History

Series Editor
Kent Deng, London School of Economics, London, UK

Palgrave Studies in Economic History is designed to illuminate and enrich our understanding of economies and economic phenomena of the past. The series covers a vast range of topics including financial history, labour history, development economics, commercialisation, urbanisation, industrialisation, modernisation, globalisation, and changes in world economic orders.

Bora Altay
Editor

Revenue-Raising Institutions, State Organization and Economic Change in the Early Modern Ottoman Empire

The Evolution of Fiscal Mechanisms, Legal Frameworks, and State Capacity

palgrave
macmillan

Editor
Bora Altay
Faculty of Political Sciences
Ankara Yıldırım Beyazıt University
Ankara, Türkiye

ISSN 2662-6497 ISSN 2662-6500 (electronic)
Palgrave Studies in Economic History
ISBN 978-3-031-96491-6 ISBN 978-3-031-96492-3 (eBook)
https://doi.org/10.1007/978-3-031-96492-3

Cover credit: Instants | Getty Images

This Palgrave Macmillan imprint is published by the registered company Springer Nature Switzerland AG
The registered company address is: Gewerbestrasse 11, 6330 Cham, Switzerland

Contents

Notes on Contributors

Bora Altay, PhD, is a faculty member of the Department of Economics at Ankara Yıldırım Beyazıt University (AYBU). He received his PhD from AYBU in 2018. His academic career started at the same university as a research assistant in 2011. Dr. Altay has focused on the long-term development and economic performance of societies. He mostly concentrates on the tools of the new institutional economics and gives particular attention to the Ottoman Empire and its institutions. Dr. Altay is the author of the book "Rules, Contracts, and Law Enforcement in the Ottoman Empire: The Case of Tax-Farming Contracts," published by Palgrave MacMillan. He is also one of the editors of the "Islamic Financial Institutions from the Early Modern Period to the 20th Century: Comparative Perspectives on the History and Development of Cash Waqfs" published by Palgrave Macmillan.

Özgür Hakan Aydoğmuş, PhD, is a faculty member at the Social Sciences University of Ankara. He received his PhD in Applied Mathematics from Iowa State University in 2013. His research focuses on modeling biological and social systems using dynamical systems and game theory. Dr. Aydoğmuş explores topics such as stochastic imitation dynamics, knowledge production, and institutional change through an evolutionary game-theoretic perspective. His recent work includes studies on the dynamics of patent pools, strategic approaches to tacit knowledge, and investment in knowledge assets.

Metin M. Coşgel is a professor of economics at the University of Connecticut, USA. He is the author of The Economics of Ottoman Justice: Settlement and Trial in the Sharia Courts (with Boğac Ergene), Cambridge University Press, 2016. He has published widely on the economic history of the Ottoman Empire, political economy of religion, and economics of social institutions. His current research interests include the long-term economic history of the Ottoman Empire and the historical roots of comparative development in the Middle East and Eastern Europe. He maintains a website on The Economic History of the Ottoman Empire (ottoman.uconn.edu).

Linda T. Darling is a professor emerita in the History Department of the University of Arizona (USA), where she taught since 1989 after receiving the PhD from the University of Chicago. Her courses covered the fields of Ottoman and Middle Eastern history, world history, and historiography. She authored *Revenue-Raising and Legitimacy: Tax Collection and Finance Administration in the Ottoman Empire, 1560–1660* (Brill 1996, electronic version 2015, Turkish translation 2019), *A History of Social Justice and Political Power in the Middle East: The Circle of Justice from Mesopotamia to Globalization* (Routledge 2013, Turkish translation 2022), and *The Janissaries of Damascus in the Sixteenth Century, or, How Conquering a Province Changed the Ottoman Empire* (EG Verlag 2019), along with many articles. She also co-edited *Reading Ottoman History: A Sourcebook* (forthcoming from Cambridge University Press) and *Festschrift for the Hoca*, a special issue of *Archivum Ottomamicum* (Vol. 38, 2021) in honor of Halil İnalcık. Her research focuses on Ottoman fiscal administration from the fourteenth to the seventeenth centuries, examining the procedures themselves, their effect on Ottoman society, and their interpretations at the hands of Ottoman and modern critics.

Erkan Gürpınar is an associate professor of Economics at the Social Sciences University of Ankara, Turkey. His main research interests are economics of knowledge, law and economics, institutional economics, evolutionary economics, and history of economic thought. He has published in a number of journals, including *Journal of Evolutionary Economics* and *Journal of Institutional Economics*.

Gencer Karabekir Karagenç is an assistant professor at the Ankara Yıldırım Beyazıt University, Faculty of Political Sciences, Department of Legal Sciences. Having completed his postgraduate education at Ankara University, Ankara Yıldırım Beyazıt University and Notthingham University, received his PhD with his thesis on the regulation of public procurement. He has many studies on various subjects of Turkish Constitutional Law and Administrative Law such as methods of providing public services, law enforcement, administrative responsibility and judicial control, international public procurement regulations, government systems, history of Turkish constitutionalism and the rule of law principal also serves on the Presidential Local Government Policies Board.

Ümit Katırancı, PhD, is a faculty member of the Department of History at Ankara Haci Bayram Veli University (HBV). He received his PhD from HBV in 2022. The subject of his doctoral dissertation was on the Candaroglu Dynasty within the Ottoman administration system. Dr. Katırancı has focused on the social and economic history of the Ottoman Empire during the fifteenth-seventeenth centuries. His research is focused on the Ottoman ruling elites, nomads, center-periphery relations, and institutions of the Ottoman Empire. He is currently working on the Ottoman ruling elites in the seventeenth century.

Hande Nur Kırmızıkuşak has been a research assistant at Yalova University since 2022. She completed her master's degree at Ankara Yıldırım Beyazıt University in 2022 and started her PhD program at Social Sciences University of Ankara in the same year. Her research interests include the economic structures of the Ottoman Empire, institutional economics, game theory, and the long-run economic performance of societies. She studies the economic structure of the Ottoman Empire and analyzes long-run inequality.

Fuat Oğuz is a retired professor of Economics with a PhD from George Mason University (2000). He has held academic positions at various universities in Turkey and visiting roles at New York University and the University of Illinois. His research focuses on law and economics, regulation, and the economics of knowledge, with publications spanning energy and telecommunications regulation, property rights, and the use of knowledge in economics.

Ramiz Üzümçeker, PhD, is a visiting lecturer at Özyeğin University, İstanbul. He earned his PhD from Boğaziçi University in 2024. His previous research focused on the economic functioning of the Ottoman pious foundations and the impact of wars on Ottoman state finances. His broader research interests include Ottoman economic history, Russian economic history, and new institutional economics.

List of Figures

List of Tables

CHAPTER 1

On the History and Structure of the Book Project

Bora Altay

This book is the result of two sessions from the initial conference series of Early Modern Ottoman Studies (EMOS), a recently established organization within The Historians Association in Ankara, Turkey. These sessions were conducted under the title 'Political Economy of State Formation: Ottoman Empire in the Long-18th Century' and were chaired by Linda Darling and Metin M. Coşgel. A notable aspect of these sessions was the significant scholarly discourse that they generated. Divergent perspectives emerged regarding the implementation of tax-farming contracts (*iltizam*), which held a prominent position in Ottoman economic history and their impact on economic performance. This book project, which synthesizes these diverse viewpoints, originates from these discussions.

B. Altay (✉)
Faculty of Political Sciences, Ankara Yıldırım Beyazıt University, Ankara, Turkey
e-mail: boraaltay@aybu.edu.tr

B. Altay (ed.), *Revenue-Raising Institutions, State Organization and Economic Change in the Early Modern Ottoman Empire*, Palgrave Studies in Economic History,
https://doi.org/10.1007/978-3-031-96492-3_1

Consequently, in contrast to individual presentations, this volume represents a reconstruction of the academic debates that occurred during these sessions.

Before delving into the academic substance of the book project, I wish to express my appreciation to several academic colleagues, who merit significant recognition. Foremost, I extend my thanks to Kayhan Orbay, whose substantial efforts in establishing the Historians' Association and bringing EMOS to fruition have provided us with this long-anticipated opportunity. Additionally, I offer my sincere gratitude to Linda Darling and Metin M. Coşgel, esteemed and experienced scholars who facilitated the discussions. I am thankful for their support with the academic dialogues and presentations, as well as their trust in contributing introductions that address both the historical and theoretical aspects of the book. Naturally, I also wish to acknowledge Fuat Oğuz, my doctoral advisor, who offered a completely novel perspective on all the historical and theoretical discussions in the conclusion. Finally, I extend my appreciation to the book's chapter authors for their support and contributions. Furthermore, I extend my gratitude to all my coworkers, who played a role in bringing the EMOS conference to fruition and exerted considerable effort to ensure that the event ran smoothly without any deficiencies.

In the early modern period, tax-farming institutions played a crucial role in state finance, administrative efficiency, and the political economy of the empires. These institutions allowed governments, such as the Ottoman Empire, France, and various Italian city-states, to secure stable revenue without the need for a large bureaucratic apparatus. By auctioning the right to collect taxes from private individuals or groups, states could immediately access liquid capital, which was essential for financing wars, maintaining military force, and sustaining large administrative structures. Tax farmers, in turn, profited from the system by collecting more than they had initially paid to the state, creating incentives for efficient but often exploitative tax collection practices. In empires like the Ottoman Empire, tax farming (*iltizam*) became a fundamental instrument for managing vast and diverse territories, reducing administrative costs while ensuring fiscal stability. However, the system also had drawbacks, as tax farmers prioritize short-term revenue maximization, which sometimes leads to higher sharecropping, social unrest, and economic inefficiency. The shift from tax farming to more centralized taxation in some regions reflected broader transformations in state capacity, institutional development, and the evolution of modern public finance systems.

Analyzing tax-farming institutions through historical approaches combined with theoretical frameworks such as game theory and new institutional economics offers significant advantages in understanding their long-term economic and political effects. From a game-theoretic perspective, tax farming can be modeled as a principal-agent problem, where the state (principal) delegates tax collection to private individuals (agents) under asymmetric information. This framework helps explain the incentives and strategic interactions among rulers, tax farmers, and taxpayers, shedding light on issues such as efficiency, corruption, and enforcement costs. It also clarifies why some tax-farming arrangements led to stable revenue flows, whereas others resulted in excessive rent extraction, economic stagnation, or political instability.

Conversely, new institutional economics provides a broader framework for analyzing tax farming as an institution shaped by transaction costs, property rights, and political actors' incentives. This approach elucidates why some societies transitioned to more efficient fiscal systems, whereas others remained dependent on extractive tax-farming arrangements. In states where strong institutional constraints and credible commitments to taxpayers emerged taxation became more predictable and conducive to long-term economic growth. In contrast, societies in which rulers lacked the ability or incentive to establish such institutions often experienced stagnation, as insecure property rights and predatory taxation discouraged investment and capital accumulation.

These approaches also contribute to broader debates about why some societies have fallen behind others in economic development. The persistence of inefficient tax-farming systems in certain regions has hindered state capacity, limited market development, and discouraged institutional reforms necessary for sustained growth. By integrating historical analysis with formal models from game theory and institutional economics, scholars can move beyond descriptive narratives to identify the underlying mechanisms that shape divergent development paths across societies. This interdisciplinary approach is crucial for understanding how institutions evolved, why some fiscal systems became more welfare-enhancing, and why certain societies struggled to transition from relatively inefficient institutional constraints.

This book consists of two main parts and 10 chapters. Except for the introductory chapter, the remaining nine chapters focus on revenue-raising institutions, state organization, and economic change in the early modern Ottoman Empire. However, these chapters are divided into two main parts. The studies in the first part focus on the history of tax collection institutions and legal regulations that emerged during the Ottoman period. The second part examines the theoretical structures of tax collection institutions that were used predominantly in the early modern period. The first part begins with Chapter 2 and this chapter presents the historical context of tax-farming institutions and provides a concise introduction of their implementation, particularly in the Ottoman Empire. Chapter 3 explores the conceptualization of tax-farming institutions in the Ottoman Empire and the integration of theoretical and historical approaches. Chapter 4 employs a historical methodology to demonstrate how tax-farming contracts were controlled by an influential family residing in Bolu, a significant city in the Ottoman Empire, using primary evidence. Chapter 5 analyzes theoretical approaches based on tax-farming contracts within the context of early modern state-building, offering a critical perspective, particularly on the concept of credible commitment, which is widely accepted in the literature. Chapter 6 examines the legal dimensions of the centralization movements that became prevalent in the Ottoman Empire during the nineteenth century and investigates the transfer of power to the center in the emergence of centralized structures from tax-farming institutions at the constitutional level. The second part of the book starts with Chapter 7 and it examines the rationale behind the practice of tax farming and introduces this historical institution through a theoretical framework. Chapter 8 uses game theory to analyze the equilibria that emerge in these contracts, employing tax-farming contracts as historical data. Chapter 9 similarly focuses on discussions of state and fiscal capacity through game-theoretic models applied to historical contracts. Chapter 10 summarizes the key findings of all discussions and presents an original proposition regarding the zero-sum logic approach to Ottoman society.

PART I

The Political Economy of Taxation in the Ottoman Past

CHAPTER 2

Introduction: A Historical Background

Linda T. Darling

The Ottoman Empire (1299–1923) is usually considered one of the great early modern empires, like the Habsburg and the Mughal. Its taxation practices, however, are descended from the medieval Mediterranean empires of the Byzantines, Seljuks, and Ilkhanids. As they made their conquests, the Ottomans adopted existing taxation practices, and during the first three centuries of their existence, they gradually modified them to bring them into harmony with each other and into conformity with their interpretations of Islamic law, justice, and precedent. Starting in the seventeenth century, greater changes were made to accommodate a monetarizing economy and a growing middle and upper class whose involvement in governance was less military but more economic in nature. Some of these changes were similar to developments elsewhere, particularly in Europe, but the differences led to a divergence of outcomes.

L. T. Darling (✉)
The University of Arizona, Tucson, AZ, US
e-mail: ldarling@arizona.edu

B. Altay (ed.), *Revenue-Raising Institutions, State Organization and Economic Change in the Early Modern Ottoman Empire*, Palgrave Studies in Economic History,
https://doi.org/10.1007/978-3-031-96492-3_2

Historic Methods of Tax Collection

Rather than a single tax on income or wealth, as in the modern world, the Ottomans taxed different economic transactions separately. Every crop grown, every item sold in the market, and many life experiences all had their own separate taxes, making tax collection something of a nightmare. Ottoman tax collection procedures, on the other hand, consisted of three sets of processes, with some overlap.[1] One process covered the taxes collected in the *timar* system, a system in which cavalry soldiers, officials, governors, and the sultan were granted rights over various revenues from the land, production, and trade in lieu of salary. *Timar*-holders or their agents collected grain and crop tithes and a few rural taxes, normally in kind, from producers and traders allotted to them by a bureaucratic process of survey and award (Inalcık 1973; Beldiceanu-Steinherr and Beldiceanu 1978, 1980). The cavalrymen were required to live on and police their allotments and to show up for military service. Promotion came with increased allotments (called *zeamets* when worth over 20,000 *akçes* and *has* over 100,000), and upper officers also acted as governors in the provinces and districts. The sultan's large allotment, amounting to about half of the revenue in this system, paid imperial expenses, and initially his personal expenses as well. Taxes owed to pious foundations were collected similarly. This system worked well until the sixteenth century, when the empire expanded beyond the original compact state and the medieval cavalry became outmoded, but there was never any systematic attempt either to reform it or to eliminate it. Instead, it was simply allowed to wither away slowly as other systems expanded their scope.

The second process was one of direct collection of taxes (*emanet*), often in cash, from those liable for them. This mode of collection was employed for the *cizye* paid by non-Muslims, tolls, and market taxes, the tax on vacant lands or on the sultan's *has*, and various occasional taxes. A collector (*emin*) and a recorder (*katib*) were sent out with a tax register (*defter*) and/or a document of command (*berat*), and they returned the money collected, minus their salaries, to the treasury along with an account. The local judge (*kadı*) exercised a supervisory role in this process. As cash taxes expanded with monetization, this system might be expected to have grown as well, but instead it was largely replaced by tax

[1] For another discussion of these kinds of taxes, see (Darling 1996a).

farming, although it was always available to be used when tax farming ran into difficulties.

Tax farming (*iltizam*), the outsourcing of tax collection to private individuals through a bidding and contractual process, was a system known in antiquity and employed by the Ottomans from the early years, mainly for taxes who totals were difficult to predict, such as bridge tolls; it was also used for the revenues of government monopolies, such as mints, rice fields, mines, and salt marshes. The Ottomans divided their revenue into sections (*mukata ʿas*), which could be collected either by *emanet* or by *iltizam*. Tax farming maximized revenue by being awarded through competitive bidding, with the tax farmer (*mültezim*) allowed to keep whatever he collected over his bid but obliged to pay any deficits out of his own pocket. For the tax farmer, it was a high-risk but high-yield investment. A tax farmer could be a single individual, a partnership, or a consortium of financiers. In difficult times, the tax farmers were required to pay their entire bid in advance. Often, they were obliged to supply guarantors (*kefils*) who would pay the tax if they defaulted. In a large iltizam, there would be a number of other employees. Ümit Katıranci's article in this volume describes how a tax farm worked.

Anyone with money, including bureaucrats, religious personnel, military men, local elites, merchants, well-to-do farmers, widows, tribal sheikhs, non-Muslims, even slaves, could bid on a tax farm by submitting a petition (*arz*) to either the imperial divan or the local *kadı* court. The complex documentation in the archives gives details of the many diverse ways in which tax farms were handled. The potential value of an *iltizam* could be determined by a prior survey or collection register, an estimate by an expert or a *kadı*, or a negotiation among the interested parties. Competitive bidding might raise the amount, and the new total could be reached by increasing production, compensating for inflation, or oppressing the taxpayers. At times when the tax farmer was unable to reach the amount bid, however, the government usually preferred to receive a lower but secure amount than to specify a higher but riskier price.

Winning a tax farming contract had implications beyond the financial. Tax farmers gained temporary *askeri* privileges and obligations, notably exposure to discretionary punishment by the sultan for non-payment of contracted amounts or oppression of the taxpayers. Once the inflation of the late sixteenth century began, making tax collection more difficult and tax farming more risky, tax farmers were able to put conditions on their bids, which consisted mainly of positions in the *askeri* for themselves, their relations, or their financial partners. The government's conditions, in turn, emphasized accurate and timely reporting and just behavior (Darling 1996a, pp. 139–140, 148–152).

Tax farming implied a certain degree of central control over the allotment of tax farms to investors, the revenues collected, and the disbursement of the collected funds, but the tax farmer's operations were performed beyond bureaucratic control. For the government, contracting out revenue collection was easier and cheaper than expanding the bureaucracy and repeating the survey procedures as often as needed, even though it demanded a relinquishment of a certain amount of control. How much control remained a source of tension between the tax farmer and the government. Mechanisms of control included surveys of expected revenues, inspection of annual accounts, cancellation of the tax farms of transgressors, and imprisonment for debt. Tax farming is usually criticized as opening the way for exploitation of the taxpayers. While the possibility always existed, government control was more stringent in the fifteenth and sixteenth centuries than it became in the seventeenth, when the tax farmers were mainly military men and provincial elites whom the government found hard to control.

As in Europe, Ottoman tax farming expanded greatly as the economy monetized. At first it encroached on direct collection, since inflation, coinage fluctuations, and popular movements rendered those taxes less predictable. It was a way for the government to transfer the uncertainties of tax collection in changing circumstances to the tax farmer. It was also widely employed to increase the income from the sultan's and high officers' portions of the *timar* taxes, which were in any case collected by agents. Eventually, lesser *timar*-holders also began to farm their allotments. In the very late seventeenth century, life-term tax farming (*malikane*) was introduced to combat the milking of tax farms by short-term collectors. It was thought that a life interest would cause tax farmers to invest their profits in the land.[2] That was mainly unsuccessful, as investment in government office brought higher rewards. In the late eighteenth century the government began taking back the tax farms and instead selling shares in the profits (similar to bonds). This move, however, was

[2] On these changes see Darling (1996b, pp. 118–131).

insufficient to stave off bankruptcy, especially after two ruinous wars with Russia in the late eighteenth century.

Tax Farming in Ottoman History

In the Ottoman Empire, tax farming was employed from the beginning for the revenues of mills, mines, customs dues, rice paddies, salt marshes, and similar taxes. The earliest surviving records come from the fifteenth century and have been studied by Furkan Taşpınar (2024, pp. 9, 147, 150–155, 160).[3] He associated tax farming with the monetization of Sultan Mehmed II (1444–46, 1451–81), and showed that it contributed a substantial amount of the cash revenue in the central treasury as well as covering payments to garrison soldiers. He found that at that time, the bidders on tax farms were merchants, moneychangers, ulema, and some Byzantine nobles, and he traced the successive bids made on specific tax farms. For example, starting in 1454, a group of mines in the Balkans were first farmed by four Muslims, possibly ulema (three were *hocas*), for four million *akçes* for three years. The next bid came two years later from one Hoca Ali, and it was for seven months for almost two million *akçes*, doubling the amount per month. One of the original tax farmers then made a bid for three years of twelve million *akçes*, three times the amount per month, but he turned out to be unable to meet that bid. He was succeeded by a Byzantine consortium, who bid eight million *akçes* for three years, slightly more than the amount the previous tax farmer had actually turned in. However, they were only able to collect three-fourths of their bid, so a new contract was made with a mixed group of tax farmers, once again for twelve million *akçes*, but given the history of this *mukata ʿa*, it is unclear why they thought they could collect that much.

An example from a century later comes from the newly conquered province of Hungary. The revenues of the *mukata ʿa* of *Vác*, covering the taxes along the river Danube everywhere except Buda/Pest, came from the customs dues of *Vác* and *Visegrád*, market taxes, court fees, and some other taxes. Customs revenue made up 85 percent of the total. In 1546 these taxes were farmed for three years for 200,000 *akçes*. A series of bidders over the next fifteen years, all Muslims and at least one a military

[3] See also Gökbilgin (1952). Important work on early tax farming has also been published in Bulgarian and Serbo-Croatian.

man, were able to raise the amount of the *iltizam* to 2,350,000 *akçes* as commerce in the region picked up after the return of peace. This figure also represented new taxes that were added to the *mukata ʿa* over that period, such as a tax on cattle, one of the biggest exports along the river.

In the published "budget" or annual account register covering the year 1495–1496, the cash received from *mukâta ʿas* in Rumeli and Anadolu added up to around 27% of the total cash revenue in the central treasury (Çakır 2016; Taşpınar 2024, pp. 29–30). That percentage increased during the first half of the sixteenth century. In the budget of 1509–1510, tax farming income amounted to nearly 40 percent of the treasury's cash revenue, and in the budget of 1524–1525, it came to more than 45 percent (Genç and Özvar 2006; Sahillioğlu 1985). According to other central treasury budgets for the sixteenth century, in 1527–28 the proportion was 63 percent, and in 1547–48 it rose to 79 percent.[4] In the second half of the century, a budget from 1567 to 1568 showed farmed revenues that only added up to 51 percent of total cash income, but in the budget of 1669–70, tax farming made up 74 percent of the treasury's cash revenue (Barkan 1957/58b; Barkan 1955/56a; Barkan 1955/56b). These percentages do not include farmed revenues sent directly to their recipients, or farmed revenues not labeled as such. Between 1568 and 1669 there are no overall figures for the level of tax farming in the empire, but there are daily log books (*ruznamçes*) that provide details. In the *ruznamçe* of 1602–3, *mukâta ʿa* revenue is calculated to have amounted to 34 percent of the total cash income (Arslanboğa 2021), but this was a period when tax collection became extremely difficult due to the Celali unrest. Further, the impression gained from examining tax farming documents from throughout the late sixteenth and early seventeenth centuries is that, over time, more different taxes were farmed, raising the proportion of farmed revenue. Overall, however, between 1560 and 1660 tax farming revenues in the central treasury budget rose only 10 percent, so their percentage of total central revenues actually decreased in real terms during that period, as inflation amounted to 225 percent (Darling 1996a, pp. 239–241).

In the classical age, the *mültezim*, the successful bidder, usually appointed himself as the *emin*, the head of the *iltizam*'s collection team. As tax farms became more complex, involving multiple *mukata ʿas* of

[4] See Barkan (1953) and Barkan (1957/58a). What caused the great leap between 1524 and 1527 is as yet unknown.

different types, the *mültezim* more often appointed others to the *emin* and *katib* positions on each *mukata ʿa*, while he stayed in the background as the financier and reaped larger rewards. He also took larger risks; due to the inflation and unrest of the late sixteenth century, the value of tax farms fluctuated wildly, and the government compensated by reducing the typical three-year term of an *iltizam* to one or less, accepting new bids without waiting for the end of a term. By the seventeenth century a one-year term was typical, although a few more stable revenue sources still had three-year terms.

In order not to lose control of tax farming, the finance department changed the process of awarding *iltizams*. One count covering 1575–1576 has 36 percent of *mültezims* coming from the military, while a register from 1603 to 1604 lists only 36 percent who were not military. By the 1620 s, *iltizams* were being granted to men who had distinguished themselves in battle, mainly men of the palace cavalry, as supplements to their salaries (Darling 1996a, pp. 179–180).[5] The prices of the *iltizams* awarded to these men did not increase, indicating that their appointment represented not a competitive bidding process but an assignment. Not only that, the treasury could compel these *mültezims* to pay in advance of collection, in the equivalent of a short term and secure loan to the treasury. On the other hand, allowing soldiers to benefit from tax farming and the associated salaries reduced unrest among the military. In the middle of the century this type of appointment diminished and the bidding process revived, as did the three-year term. Subsequently, the revenues of provinces began to be farmed, with the governors as *mültezims* undertaking to submit a certain amount of provincial revenue to the treasury (Inalcık 1977, pp. 29–30; Kunt 1983; Murphey 1979, pp. 202–203). The introduction of *malikane* (life-term tax farming) in 1695 further extended the use of tax farming, making it the characteristic form of tax collection for the eighteenth century (Genç 1975).

Conclusion

The articles in this book refer mainly to the subsequent period of the eighteenth and nineteenth centuries, when tax farming was by far the dominant form of tax collection in the Ottoman Empire. In that period,

[5] At the same time, the military began to dominate *cizye* collection.

the tax farmers were mostly provincial and central elites and Janissaries, and tax farms were mostly large conglomerates of income sources. The tax farmers regarded tax farming as a route to bountiful income, powerful influence, and control of territories, people, and economic processes. It is important to understand their aims, their options, and the costs of their endeavors. By this time, tax farming had become much more complex than the relatively simple form it took in the fifteenth century. However, the stresses and opportunities remained. These studies are designed to throw light on the similarities and differences of late Ottoman tax farming with its own past and with other tax farming systems.

References

Arslanboğa, K. (2021). Revenues and Expenses of the Central Treasury of the Ottoman Empire for the Fiscal Year of 1602–1603. In A. Ç. Ceylan, M. B. Kurt, and Z. Özomay (Eds.), *Research and Reviews in Social Human and Administrative Sciences*. Gece Kitaplığı.

Barkan, Ö. L. (1953). H. 933–934 (M 1527–1528) Mali Yılına Ait Bütçe Örneği. *İstanbul Üniversitesi İktisat Fakültesi Mecmuasi (İÜİFM)* 14, 251–329.

Barkan, Ö. L. (1955/56a). 1079–1080 (1669–1670) Mâli Yılına âit Bir Osmanlı Bütçesi ve Ek'leri. *İstanbul Üniversitesi İktisat Fakültesi Mecmuasi (İÜİFM)* 17, 225–303.

Barkan, Ö. L. (1955/56b). 1070–1071 (1660–1661) Tarihli Osmanlı Bütçesi ve Bir Mukayese. *İstanbul Üniversitesi İktisat Fakültesi Mecmuasi (İÜİFM)* 17, 304–347.

Barkan, Ö. L. (1957/58a). H. 954–955 (1547–1548) Malî Yılına âit bir Osmanlı Bütçesi. Mali Yılına Ait Bütçe Örneği. *İstanbul Üniversitesi İktisat Fakültesi Mecmuasi (İÜİFM)* 19, 219–276.

Barkan, Ö. L. (1957/58b). H. 974–975 (M. 1567–1568) Malî Yılına âit bir Osmanlı Bütçesi. *İstanbul Üniversitesi İktisat Fakültesi Mecmuasi (İÜİFM)* 19, 277–332.

Beldiceanu-Steinherr, I. and Beldiceanu, N. (1978). Règlement Ottoman Concernant le Recensement (Première Moitié du XVIe Siècle). *Südost-Forschungen* 39, 1–40.

Beldiceanu-Steinherr, I. and Beldiceanu, N. (1980). *Le Timar dans l'état Ottoman (début XIVe-début XVIe Siècle)*. Otto Harrassowitz.

Çakır, B. (2016). Osmanlı Devleti'nin Bilinen En Eski (1495–1496) Bütçesi ve 1494–1496 Yılı İcmali. *The Journal of Ottoman Studies* 47, 113–145.

Darling, L. (1996a). *Revenue-Rising and Legitimacy: Tax Collection and Finance Administration in the Ottoman Empire, 1560–1660*. Brill.

Darling, L. (1996b). Public Finances: The Role of the Ottoman Centre. In S. Faroqhi (Ed.), *The Cambridge History of Turkey, vol. 3: The Later Ottoman Empire, 1603–1838*. Cambridge University Press.

Genç, M. (1975). Osmanlı Maliyesinde Malikane Sistemi. In O. Okyar and H.Ü. Nalbantoğlu (Eds.), *Türkiye İktisat Tarihi Semineri: Metinler-Tartışmalar*. Hacettepe Üniversitesi Yayınları.

Genç, M. and Özvar, Ö. (Eds.) (2006). *Osmanlı Maliyesi: Kurumlar ve Bütçeler, v.2*. Osmanlı Bankası Arşiv ve Araştırma Merkezi.

Gökbilgin, M. T. (1952). *XV.–XVI. Asırlarda Edirne ve Paşa Livası: Vakıflar—Mülkler—Mukataalar*. Üçler Basımevi.

Inalcık, H. (1973). *The Ottoman Empire: The Classical Age*. Weidenfeld and Nicolson.

Inalcık, H. (1977). Centralization and Decentralization in Ottoman Administration. In T. Naff and R. Owen (Eds.), *Studies in Eighteenth Century Islamic History*. Southern Illinois University Press.

Kunt, M. (1983). *The Sultan's Servants: The Transformation of Ottoman Provincial Government, 1550–1650*. Columbia University Press.

Murphey, R. (1979). *The Functioning of the Ottoman Army under Murad IV (1623–39/1032–1049): Key to the Understanding of the Relationship between Center and Periphery in Seventeenth-Century Turkey*. PhD dissertation, University of Chicago.

Sahillioğlu, H. (1985). 1524–1525 Osmanli Bütçesi. *İstanbul Üniversitesi İktisat Fakültesi Mecmuasi (İÜİFM)* 14, 415–449.

Taşpınar, F. (2024). *An Early Monetization? Tracing the Mukâtaʿa System Back to the Reign of Mehmed II*. MA Thesis, İhsan Doğramacı Bilkent University, Ankara.

CHAPTER 3

Conceptualization of Ottoman Institutions: A Brief Review for Theoretical Assessment of Tax-Farming Contracts

Bora Altay

The Ottoman Empire, one of the most enduring and influential empires in world history, persisted for over six centuries and governed extensive territories across Europe, Asia, and Africa. The empire's institutional framework was both intricate and dynamic, evolving in response to diverse political, economic, and social pressures. Among these institutions, the tax-farming institution (known as iltizam) emerged as one of the key mechanisms for revenue collection and state finance management throughout the early modern period. Tax farming, through which the Ottoman state delegated tax collection to private contractors, enabled the empire to generate revenue, while circumventing the costs of direct bureaucratic control. However, this system also became a source of

B. Altay (✉)
Faculty of Political Sciences, Ankara Yıldırım Beyazıt University, Ankara, Turkey
e-mail: boraaltay@aybu.edu.tr

B. Altay (ed.), *Revenue-Raising Institutions, State Organization and Economic Change in the Early Modern Ottoman Empire*, Palgrave Studies in Economic History,
https://doi.org/10.1007/978-3-031-96492-3_3

contention, raising questions about efficiency, legitimacy, and the extent of centralized authority. Theoretical analyses of tax-farming contracts in the context of Ottoman institutions yield crucial insights into how states in pre-modern economies balanced fiscal requirements, governance structures, and their relationships with society. As Abou-El-Haj (2000, p. 124) emphasized, Ottoman institutions need to be addressed from different perspectives, and different research methods are required to examine political change and economic and social interests from a methodological perspective. This approach requires focusing on the internal dynamics of the Ottoman Empire, especially in the early modern period. The examination of the internal dynamics presented by historical primary sources using new models and approaches offers new and original contributions to the literature. This study also suggests different alternatives and methods for these contributions based on different problems.

The central problem addressed in this study is the inefficiency and sustainability of the Ottoman tax-farming system, which, while enabling the empire to function without a costly central bureaucracy, also created systemic weaknesses. These weaknesses, particularly in the form of contracting, local autonomy, and inequality, ultimately undermined the empire's fiscal stability. It is improbable that these weaknesses were not genuine limitations of this period. The empire's relatively expansive geography, compared to other states, presents challenges in implementing the transformations such as bureaucratic structures and representative bodies discussed in the literature (Johnson 2006; Balla and Johnson 2009; Johnson and Koyama 2014; Altay and Oğuz 2021). Therefore, transformations aimed at enhancing state and fiscal capacity may have been costlier for the Ottoman Empire; thus, it can be posited that the mechanisms employed were effective and sustainable equilibria (Salzmann 1993, 2004; Darling 1996; İnalcık 2000; Genç 2000). Despite its central role in Ottoman governance, tax farming has received limited comprehensive theoretical scrutiny, particularly in comparison to other early modern tax systems in Europe and other regions. Furthermore, the principal-agent dynamics of tax-farming contracts in the Ottoman Empire remain underexplored, especially in relation to how they shaped the empire's ability to mobilize resources, maintain coercive authority, and navigate the complexities of decentralized governance.

This study is significant for several reasons. First, it elucidates a crucial aspect of Ottoman governance that is fundamental to comprehending the empire's fiscal and administrative development. The Ottoman tax-farming system constituted not only a vital economic institution but also a lens through which to examine the broader mechanisms of state capacity and political organization in early modern empires. By analyzing tax-farming contracts through contemporary theoretical frameworks, particularly principal-agent theory, this study offers a more nuanced understanding of the interaction between central authority and local agents. Second, a comparative analysis of tax-farming systems in France, England, and other contemporary regimes reveals both the commonalities and distinctive features of the Ottoman system, thereby contributing to our understanding of state-building and institutional resilience in non-Western contexts. Finally, this study engages with longstanding debates in Ottoman economic history, presenting novel perspectives on the relationship between the state, its elites, and the general populace, while challenging conventional assumptions regarding Ottoman decline, fiscal crisis, and institutional inertia.

The contributions of this study are multifaceted. First, it provides a theoretical assessment of tax-farming contracts in the Ottoman Empire, utilizing modern institutional economics and principal-agent analysis. This approach facilitates a more comprehensive understanding of the incentives, behaviors, and constraints faced by both Ottoman state and tax farmers. This study posits that the inefficiencies inherent in the system were a result of the asymmetry of information and moral hazards engendered by the contracts, a dynamic that has not been fully elucidated in previous historical analyses. Second, it contributes to the comparative literature on early modern tax systems, particularly by focusing on the Ottoman case (Kiser 1987, 1994; Kiser and Kane 2001; Kiser and Linton 2001; Coşgel and Miceli 2009; Johnson and Koyama 2014; Altay and Oğuz 2021). By contrasting the Ottoman tax-farming system with those of France, England, and Prussia, this research elucidates the key differences in state capacity, bureaucratic structure, and the role of local elites. These comparisons serve to contextualize the advantages and disadvantages of decentralized fiscal arrangements in a historical setting, offering broader implications for understanding the development of state institutions across different regions. Finally, this study challenges the prevailing narratives on Ottoman decline by demonstrating how the inherent contradictions in the tax-farming system, specifically the tension between central authority and local autonomy, exacerbated the empire's fiscal difficulties.

It posits that these contradictions were not merely the result of administrative inefficiencies but were deeply embedded in the institutional design of tax-farming contracts, reflecting more profound issues of governance and legitimacy.

This study is structured into several key arguments. First, it posits that the Ottoman tax-farming system, as a principal-agent perspective and contract choices, operated on the principles of delegation and trust, wherein the central state relied on local elites for tax collection. While providing short-term benefits, this delegation engendered long-term inefficiency, opportunism, and political fragmentation. Second, the study demonstrates that the institutional design of tax-farming contracts in the Ottoman Empire was characterized by informational asymmetry and moral hazard, which generated incentives for opportunistic behaviors and undermined the empire's capacity to adapt to changing economic and political conditions. Third, it contends that while the system allowed for flexibility and cost-effectiveness in the short term, its inherent contradictions established a foundation for fiscal crises and political instability in the long term. Finally, a comparative analysis with European tax systems elucidates the Ottoman Empire's distinctive approach to decentralized governance, underscoring the limitations and potential pitfalls of the tax-farming model when implemented in a complex and dynamic political environment.

In subsequent sections, this study presents a comprehensive analysis of the literature and theoretical frameworks that underpinned the tax-farming system in the Ottoman Empire, compares these arrangements with European models, and evaluates the long-term implications of this institutional structure for the empire's fiscal and political trajectory. This examination offers a novel perspective on Ottoman institutional development and provides significant insights into the broader processes of state formation and institutional change in early modern history.

Literature Review: Tax-Farming in the Ottoman Empire and Other European States

The tax-farming institution played a key role in the Ottoman Empire's governance and fiscal strategy, serving as a critical link between the central authority and provincial administration. Scholars have long recognized its significance as a mechanism for revenue generation; however, its implications for state capacity, governance structures, and economic stability remain subjects of ongoing debate. By outsourcing tax collection to private individuals or entities, the Ottoman state reduced administrative costs, while managing a vast and diverse empire. Nevertheless, this decentralization also presented challenges, including opportunism, inefficiency, and local autonomy, which at times undermined the central authority. The literature on Ottoman tax farming, particularly when examined through contemporary theoretical frameworks such as principal-agent theory and historical experiences, offers valuable insights into these dynamics, and provides a comparative lens with other early modern states. This review synthesizes key contributions from the literature, highlighting the strengths and limitations of tax farming in the Ottoman context, and situating them within broader debates on state formation and institutional development.

The Ottoman Empire's approach to governance and economic management, particularly through tax farming, demonstrated a system of adaptive governance that evolved in response to shifting political and economic challenges. Tax farming, a revenue collection mechanism whereby private individuals or entities collect taxes in exchange for fixed payments to the state, played a crucial role in the administration of one of the world's most enduring empires. The existing literature examined the historical trajectory of tax farming in the Ottoman Empire, emphasizing its adaptive characteristics, broader implications for state-society relations.

Tax farming's origins in the Ottoman Empire could be traced to its formative years, with institutional antecedents in earlier Islamic and Byzantine traditions. According to Karaman and Pamuk (2010), the Ottoman state implemented tax farming as a pragmatic response to its extensive territorial acquisitions and concomitant necessity for efficient revenue collection. The timar system, an early manifestation of tax farming, allocated land revenue to cavalry soldiers (*sipahis*) in exchange for military services. By the sixteenth century, the transition to cash-based taxation had necessitated institutional innovation. The tax-farming institution emerged; wherein *mültezims* (private contractors) bid for the right to collect taxes. This mechanism provided a state with annual installments, thereby reducing fiscal uncertainty, while transferring the risks of tax collection to the mültezims. Linda Darling (1996) provided an in-depth examination of how this system integrated fiscal needs with administrative flexibility. This research emphasized that the tax-farming institution not only provided immediate liquidity to the state, but also incentivized mültezims to maximize tax-collection efficiency, albeit with significant social and economic implications.

The evolution of tax farming reflected the Ottoman state's adaptability to external and internal pressure. In the seventeenth century, the empire faced increasing military expenditures, declines in territorial expansion, and inflationary pressures driven by the influx of New World silver. Murat Çizakça (1996) and Mehmet Genç (2000) posited that the central administration responded by expanding the tax-farming contracts, frequently granting lifetime tax-farming contracts (*malikane*). This innovation stabilized revenue streams and encouraged long-term investments in local economies. Çizakça (1996)'s analysis further elucidates how the lifetime contracts represented a significant shift in governance. By granting lifetime contracts, the state cultivated a quasi-partnership with provincial elites. While the new form ensured a reliable flow of revenue, it also facilitated the accumulation of local power and wealth, occasionally at the expense of central authority. Darling (1996) observed that this decentralization was both a strength and vulnerability, reflecting the Ottoman state's reliance on negotiated authority.

The efficacy and limitations of tax farming are inextricably linked to the broader political economy of the Ottoman Empire. Mehmet Genç (2000) emphasizes that tax farming reflected the state's pragmatic approach to governance, which balanced fiscal efficiency with social legitimacy. By co-opting provincial elites through tax-farming contracts, the central administration mitigated the costs of direct governance in extensive and diverse territories. Darling (1996) contributes to this understanding by emphasizing the role of legitimacy in sustaining the tax-farming system. This study posits that the state's capacity to mediate disputes and ensure equitable tax practices was crucial in maintaining its authority over both mültezims and the broader populace.

Ottoman reliance on tax farming represents an alternative trajectory to the centralized bureaucracies that emerged in Western Europe during the early modern period. Scholars have emphasized the flexibility of the Ottoman system, which contributed to its longevity but also limited its capacity for modernization (Pamuk 2004a, 2004b). This contrast elucidates unique challenges faced by empires with diverse populations and expansive territories. In the eighteenth century, privatization trends further transformed the Ottoman political economy. Tax farming facilitated the ascendance of provincial elites, altering the balance between central and local authorities (Çizakça 1989, p. 67; Genç 2000, pp. 113–114; Abou-El-Haj 2000, pp. 80–89; Pamuk 2000, p. 110; Karaman 2009, p. 695; Tezcan 2010, p. 17; Yaycıoğlu 2016, p. 67; İnalcık 2017, p. 65). While this privatization provided short-term stability, it also entrenched local power structures, complicating efforts to centralize governance. The tensions between provincial autonomy and centralized reform became particularly pronounced during the nineteenth-century Tanzimat era, when the state sought to modernize fiscal and administrative practices. Comparative studies of tax farming in other early modern empires underscore the trade-offs between decentralization and fiscal control (Ashton 1956; Bonney 1979; Kiser 1987; Kiser an Kane 2001; White 2004; Drelichman and Voth 2011; Johnson and Koyama 2017; Ma and Rubin 2019). These analyses situate the Ottoman experience within a broader context, illuminating the implications of tax farming for state-building and the institutional evolution in pre-modern states.

By the nineteenth century, the Ottoman Empire's reliance on tax farming began to diminish as modern bureaucratic states and global economic integration reshaped governance structures. The Tanzimat reforms marked a decisive shift toward direct taxation and state-managed revenue collection. These reforms aimed to centralize authority and modernize fiscal institutions, positioning the empire to compete with European powers. The decline in tax farming illustrates the challenges of transitioning from a decentralized system to a centralized bureaucratic model. The erosion of provincial autonomy and the increasing demands of the modern state created tensions that reshaped Ottoman governance in the final century. This transformation encompassed the professionalization of administrative functions, standardization of taxation practices, and assertion of greater control over provinces, fundamentally altering the relationship between the state and society.

The historical evolution of tax farming in the Ottoman Empire provides a nuanced case study on adaptive governance. By utilizing decentralized revenue collection mechanisms, the Ottoman state navigated centuries of political and economic change. However, the trade-offs inherent in this system—between central authority and local autonomy, and efficiency—elucidate the complexities of institutional design in a pre-modern context. This examination reveals enduring lessons regarding the interplay between fiscal practices, political legitimacy, and institutional resilience. The Ottoman experience, augmented by comparative insights, demonstrates how states can adapt to shifting challenges while contending with the inherent tensions of decentralization. Situating the Ottoman system within a global framework offers valuable perspectives on governance and institutional evolution in the early modern empires.

Theoretical Foundations: Principal-Agent Dynamics

Tax farming, a method by which the state outsources tax collection to private individuals or entities, has been a significant component of the economic and administrative history. In this system, the state (the principal) delegates responsibility for tax collection to tax farmers (agents), who are remunerated based on the revenue they collect. This delegation of responsibility is inherently fraught with conflicts of interest, which are best understood through the principal-agent theory. The principal-agent framework elucidates how the differing incentives between the state and the tax farmers influence economic outcomes, including the efficiency of tax collection and its broader effects on economic performance. This chapter elaborates on the principal-agent dynamics in tax farming, exploring its theoretical underpinnings, and explains why principal-agent models are crucial for comprehending tax farming's implications for state capacity and economic performance.

Principal-agent theory provides a framework to elucidate the relationship between the state and the tax farmer, wherein the state (the principal) engages the tax farmer (the agent) to collect taxes. The primary challenge lies in aligning an agent's interests with those of the principal. In a tax-farming system, the principal (the state) aims to maximize revenue and ensure efficient tax collection, whereas the agent (the tax farmer) aims to maximize personal profit. This divergence of interests constitutes the fundamental issue of the principal-agent problem. Tax farmers, motivated by their self-interest, may engage in behaviors that conflict with the state's objectives, such as excessive taxation of the population, underreporting of collections, or implementation of coercive strategies.

Principal-agent theory elucidates several key issues that arise from these conflicting interests: moral hazard, asymmetric information, monitoring challenges, and contract design (Kiser 1994). The state's capacity to mitigate these issues is contingent on its ability to effectively monitor tax farmers, structure contracts that align incentives, and ensure compliance. These concepts are fundamental to comprehending the broader dynamics of tax farming, which have historically had significant implications for the efficacy of tax systems and the state's economic performance.

Principal-agent models are essential for comprehending tax farming, as they provide a robust framework for analyzing the underlying incentives and dynamics between the state and tax farmers in the early modern Ottoman Empire (Altay and Oğuz 2021). The application of these models elucidates how agency costs arising from an agent's self-interested behavior can engender inefficiencies in tax collection, which subsequently impacts broader economic performance. First, the principal-agent model elucidates the misalignment of incentives between the state and tax farmer. The state aims to maximize long-term tax revenue while maintaining social stability, whereas tax farmers are motivated by short-term profit maximization. This misalignment results in behaviors such as overextraction, opportunism, and rent-seeking. Through the analysis of these incentives, principal-agent models facilitate the identification of risks inherent in tax farming and the mechanisms by which these risks can compromise the efficiency of the tax system.

Second, inefficient tax systems due to principal-agent problems have significant consequences for economic performance. When tax farmers extract excessive rent, they can lead to economic stagnation by reducing the resources available for investment and innovation. Excessive taxation or the use of coercive tactics can inhibit economic activity, particularly in the agricultural and commercial sectors, as individuals are disincentivized from engaging in productive economic activities. The failure to collect taxes efficiently can also reduce the state's revenue, which in turn limits its ability to fund public goods and services that are essential for long-term economic growth. Principal-agent theory elucidates how these inefficiencies arise from poorly structured contracts, inadequate monitoring, and the self-interest of tax farmers. In this manner, the model provides a framework through which to understand the long-term economic consequences of tax-farming systems and how they can impede economic development.

Finally, the principal-agent model is valuable for understanding the relationship between state capacity and governance. The state's ability to effectively manage tax farmers through monitoring and enforcement is directly linked to its administrative capacity. Principal-agent theory helps to conceptualize how states with weak administrative structures struggle to manage the agency costs associated with tax farming. In such cases, the state is less able to ensure that tax farmers fulfill their duties responsibly, which leads to higher levels of abuse, inefficiency, and opportunism. Conversely, principal-agent theory also explains why states with stronger bureaucracies are more capable of designing effective contracts and monitoring mechanisms that reduce the risks of agency costs. This theoretical insight is important for understanding the role of state capacity in shaping economic performance, as the ability to collect taxes efficiently and deploy public resources is fundamental to achieving sustained economic growth and political stability.

The principal-agent dynamics in tax farming are influenced by several key factors, each of which contributes to the efficiency of the system. These include moral hazard (rent-seeking), asymmetric information, monitoring challenges, and contract design. First, the principal problem in tax farming, as elucidated by the principal-agent theory, is moral hazard or rent-seeking behavior. Tax farmers, cognizant that their remuneration is contingent upon the revenue they collect, are incentivized to over extract, or employ coercive measures to maximize their profits. This engenders a situation in which the agent's conduct may undermine the principal's objective. In the context of tax farming, moral hazard is further exacerbated by the fixed nature of the lump-sum payment, or the proportion of revenue retained by the tax farmer, which may lead to short-term maximization at the expense of long-term system stability. This dynamic can be detrimental not only to the populace but also to the state itself, as excessive taxation and opportunism reduce compliance and distort economic incentives, potentially resulting in lower overall tax revenues in the long term (Altay and Oğuz 2021, p. 42). By employing principal-agent theory to analyze these behaviors, we can identify how and why moral hazard undermines the efficacy of tax systems.

Second, in a tax-farming arrangement, tax farmers typically possess superior information compared to the state regarding local economic conditions, the tax base, and the population's ability to pay. This information asymmetry creates an environment in which tax farmers can manipulate the tax system to their advantage. Asymmetric information increases the likelihood of underreporting or misreporting the amount of taxes collected, making it challenging for the state to assess the effectiveness of the tax-farming system. Principal-agent models emphasize how these informational disparities can lead to inefficiencies in the tax-collection process, as the state is unable to effectively monitor or verify the actions of tax farmers. This results in a situation where the tax system may appear to be functioning efficiently on paper but is, in reality, yielding less revenue and causing more detriment to the population than is publicly acknowledged.

Third, the ability of the state to monitor and enforce tax collection is a critical component in managing principal-agent problems. Principal-agent theory provides insight into how monitoring and enforcement mechanisms can be designed to mitigate agency costs. However, monitoring is often costly and challenging, particularly in large, decentralized, or resource-constrained states. When monitoring is inadequate or inefficient, tax farmers can operate with minimal concern for repercussions, which results in increased inefficiency and abuse. From the perspective of principal-agent theory, it is evident that the state's administrative capacity plays a crucial role in determining the efficacy or failure of tax farming. The more effective the state's monitoring and enforcement mechanisms, the less probable it is that tax farmers will exploit their position for personal gain (Ma and Rubin 2019). The theory thus elucidates how variations in state capacity can lead to divergent outcomes in tax-farming systems, ranging from inefficiency and opportunism to more effective revenue collection.

Fourth, the design of the contract between the state and tax farmer is crucial for aligning the incentives of both parties. Principal-agent theory states that the structure of a contract can exacerbate or mitigate the risks of moral hazard, asymmetric information, and rent-seeking. The state can endeavor to reduce agency costs by designing contracts with performance-based elements, such as revenue-sharing clauses, periodic audits, or stringent penalties for underreporting. However, such contracts are only efficacious if the state possesses the capacity to enforce them and tax farmers are sufficiently incentivized to comply. A well-designed contract should provide tax farmers with adequate incentives to collect taxes efficiently while ensuring that the state's revenue objectives are met. Principal-agent models facilitate the understanding of the trade-offs involved in contract design and the mechanisms by which states can utilize incentives to manage their relationships with tax farmers. By analyzing the structure of tax-farming contracts through a principal-agent framework, one can identify strategies that minimize the risks of abuse and enhance the efficiency of tax collection.

Principal-agent models provide a valuable framework for elucidating the intricacies of tax-farming systems and their implications for economic performance. By examining the incentive structures, information asymmetries, and monitoring challenges inherent in the principal-agent relationship, these models offer substantive insights into the mechanisms by which tax-farming systems frequently result in inefficiencies, opportunistic behavior, and diminished state capacity. Furthermore, they elucidate the broader economic ramifications of such systems, including their impacts on economic growth, stability, and governance. The application of principal-agent theory to the analysis of tax farming facilitates a more comprehensive understanding of the operational dynamics of these systems, their potential shortcomings, and potential avenues for reform to better align the interests of the state and its agents, thereby potentially enhancing economic performance.

Contracting Tax Farming in the Ottoman Empire: Markets and Hierarcies

As previously noted, tax farming played a crucial role in the fiscal system of the Ottoman Empire, functioning as a mechanism for revenue collection, while addressing the administrative challenges presented by a vast and diverse empire. In this system, the state delegated the responsibility for tax collection to private individuals or entities in exchange for a predetermined payment or share of revenue. Over time, the Ottoman tax-farming system evolved through a combination of market-driven competitive contracts and hierarchical bureaucratic allocation. These distinct forms of tax-farming contracts reflect the empire's efforts to balance efficiency, revenue maximization, and administrative control. This section examines the dynamics of contracting tax farming in the Ottoman Empire by drawing on insights from historical tax-collection mechanisms. Through an analysis of the market and hierarchical forms of tax farming, this section aims to elucidate the institutional logic underlying these practices and their implications for the Ottoman fiscal and administrative structure as well as the broader economic and social ramifications of these systems.

The theoretical foundation for understanding tax-farming contracts lies in the distinction between market and hierarchical forms of governance. As conceptualized by Kiser (1994), market forms rely on competitive mechanisms in which multiple agents bid for contracts, thereby ensuring that the most capable and efficient tax farmers are selected. By contrast, hierarchical forms are characterized by centralized bureaucratic allocation, wherein the state assigns contracts based on administrative decisions rather than competitive bidding. Both forms present distinct advantages and limitations that are particularly relevant to the Ottoman context.

Competitive contracts incentivize efficiency by fostering competition among potential tax farmers. Tax farmers who submit the highest bids demonstrate their capacity to generate revenue by aligning their interests with those of the state. The selection process diminishes the necessity for extensive state oversight, because competitive mechanisms inherently reward capable agents. However, the emphasis on short-term profitability can result in overextraction and social unrest as tax farmers endeavor to rapidly recover their initial investments. Bureaucratic allocation relies on a state's administrative capacity to identify and appoint suitable agents based on loyalty, competence, or connections. This approach allows the state to exercise greater control over tax collection, mitigating the risks of overextraction and reducing the likelihood of social instability. It promotes long-term stability and sustainability, as tax farmers are often incentivized to maintain the productivity of their tax base. However, this method requires a robust bureaucratic infrastructure and may be susceptible to inefficiencies or favoritism, particularly in the absence of effective oversight mechanisms.

The Ottoman Empire's approach to tax farming exemplifies a hybrid system incorporating both market and hierarchical elements (Coşgel and Miceli 2009). The selection of these forms was influenced by the empire's administrative capacity, geographic constraints, fiscal priorities, and evolving requirements of the state over time. The tax-farming institution, prevalent during the classical period of the Ottoman Empire, epitomized the market form of tax farming. Under this system, tax-farming contracts were auctioned to the highest bidder, often for a specified period, typically one to three years. The competitive nature of tax-farming institution ensured that the state secured the maximum possible revenue upfront, as tax farmers remitted a lump sum in advance to obtain the rights to collect taxes. This immediate infusion of funds was particularly advantageous during periods of fiscal strain such as wartime or in the aftermath of natural disasters. Tax farmers under the tax-farming institution were granted considerable autonomy, which allowed them to optimize their operations and adapt to local conditions. However, this autonomy also meant that the state had limited direct control over the tax farmers' actions. The reliance on competitive bidding introduced the risk of over-taxation, as tax farmers sought to recover their initial investment and generate profits. This has frequently resulted in social unrest, economic stagnation, and resentment among the taxed population.

By the late seventeenth century, the Ottoman Empire initiated a transition to lifetime contracts that incorporated hierarchical elements while retaining aspects of market allocation. This system involved granting lifetime tax-farming contracts to individuals or institutions, often based on their financial capabilities, loyalty, or administrative qualifications. While maintaining an auction component, these contracts emphasize long-term revenue stability rather than short-term maximization. The lifetime contracts reduced the frequency of auctions and short-term focus of tax-farming contracts, thereby promoting greater stability and continuity in tax collection. Lifetime contracts incentivized tax farmers to invest in the productivity and sustainability of their tax base, as their tenure depended on sustained revenue generation. This approach aligned the interests of tax farmers with those of the state, fostering cooperation with local populations and contributing to the stability of the tax base. However, the hierarchical aspects of the lifetime contracts did not eliminate challenges entirely. The process of allocating contracts occasionally creates opportunities for favoritism and opportunism. Additionally, the entrenchment of powerful tax farmers or institutions periodically poses challenges to the central authority of the state. Despite these limitations, the lifetime contracts represented a strategic adaptation by the Ottoman state, blending market, and bureaucratic principles to suit its fiscal and administrative priorities.

From this perspective, the question of why the Ottoman Empire adhered to the auction system, called the market form, is significant. The Ottoman Empire's reliance on market forms and auction mechanisms to allocate tax-farming contracts can be attributed to several interconnected factors that align with the state's fiscal priorities, administrative capabilities, and institutional strategies. By employing market-based systems, the Empire sought to optimize its revenue collection while addressing the structural and logistical challenges inherent in governing a vast and diverse territory. The primary reasons for this are fiscal imperatives and the need for immediate revenue. One of the principal factors in the prevalence of auction-based mechanisms in tax farming was the empire's consistent need for immediate cash flows. The *Iltizam* system, wherein tax-farming rights were granted to the highest bidder, provided an efficient means of generating substantial upfront payments. These lump-sum payments were crucial during military campaigns, infrastructure projects, and economic crises. The competitive bidding process ensured that the state could maximize its fiscal returns with minimal delays. Unlike hierarchical forms of revenue collection, which require significant investments in bureaucratic capacity and long-term institutional oversight, the market-oriented allocation delivered immediate fiscal benefits. The predictability and regularity of revenue inflows from auctions reduced the state's financial uncertainty, enabling it to plan its expenditure more effectively.

The second reason is the potential for enhanced efficiency through competition facilitated by the vast territories of the empire. The utilization of auctions ensures a certain degree of efficiency in the selection of tax farmers. By establishing a competitive environment, the state could identify agents willing to offer the highest price for tax-farming rights, which often correlates with their perceived ability to generate revenue from the designated region. This competitive selection process minimized the administrative burden on the state, as it relied on market forces to identify the most capable candidates without necessitating extensive bureaucratic evaluations. Furthermore, competition among bidders incentivizes innovation and tax-collection efficiency. Tax farmers who secured contracts through auctions were motivated to implement strategies that maximized revenue extraction, as their profits depended on surpassing the costs they had committed to the state. This alignment of incentives allowed the Ottoman state to delegate tax-collection responsibilities without directly intervening in operational details.

The third reason is administrative limitations and decentralized governance within the institutional environment. The vast territorial expanse and ethnically diverse population of the Ottoman Empire present significant administrative challenges. Establishing a centralized bureaucratic system capable of directly overseeing tax collection in all regions would have necessitated a level of institutional capacity and resources that the state was either unwilling or unable to commit. Market-based mechanisms such as auctions effectively address these limitations by decentralizing the tax-collection process. By delegating tax collection to private individuals or entities, the state could leverage local expertise and networks without expanding its bureaucratic apparatus. Tax farmers, often drawn from local elites or individuals with established connections in their regions, possess intimate knowledge of local economic conditions and social dynamics. This decentralized approach reduced administrative costs and enabled the state to extend its fiscal reach to peripheral areas, which would have been challenging to govern directly.

The fourth reason can be attributed to the adaptability of tax-farming contracts and risk-management strategies. Market-oriented tax-farming contracts provided the Ottoman state with a flexible and adaptive system for revenue collection. The short-term nature of Iltizam contracts allowed the state to recalibrate its fiscal policies and adjust contract terms based on fluctuating economic, political, or social circumstances. This adaptability was particularly advantageous in an empire characterized by regional variations and dynamic economic conditions. Furthermore, auctions enabled the state to transfer a significant portion of the financial risk associated with the tax collection to private agents. Tax farmers assumed responsibility for meeting the state's revenue expectations regardless of fluctuations in local economic productivity or tax compliance. This arrangement mitigated the state's exposure to revenue shortfalls and ensured a consistent stream of income even during periods of economic instability.

The fifth reason is reliance on institutional legacy and path dependence within the institutional environment. The historical development of tax farming in the Ottoman Empire contributed to the continued prevalence of market-based mechanisms. The tax-farming institution was deeply integrated into the fiscal and administrative structure of the state in the early modern period. Transitioning to a fully hierarchical form of tax collection would have necessitated the radical restructuring of existing institutions and practices, potentially disrupting the established power dynamics and risking opposition from influential stakeholders. The auction-based system, with its demonstrated effectiveness in generating revenue and maintaining administrative stability, represents a path-dependent choice that reinforces its persistence. The state's utilization of these mechanisms was further justified by their alignment with the broader economic and political context of the era, which prioritized expediency and pragmatism over long-term institutional transformation.

The sixth reason is predicated on social and political considerations. The utilization of market forms in tax-farming allocation also reflects Ottoman state's cognition of the social and political implications of its fiscal policies. By involving local elites and influential tax farmers, the state was able to co-opt potential sources of opposition and integrate them into the administrative framework. This strategy not only reduced the likelihood of rebellion, but also strengthened the legitimacy of the state's authority in the perception of local populations. Auctions served as a mechanism for balancing the interests of the central state with those of the regional actors. By granting tax-farming rights through competitive bidding, the state maintained a degree of control over the process, while accommodating the participation of local stakeholders. This delicate equilibrium helped sustain the Empire's administrative cohesion and minimized the potential for conflicts arising from fiscal governance.

Therefore, the Ottoman Empire's preference for market forms and auctions in allocating tax-farming contracts was a pragmatic response to the fiscal, administrative, and political challenges that it faced. By leveraging competitive mechanisms, the state was able to generate immediate revenue, enhance efficiency, and mitigate the risks associated with direct tax collection. These market-oriented practices also reflected the Empire's broader institutional strategies, which prioritized adaptability and decentralization in navigating the complexities of governing a vast and diverse territory. Through its reliance on auctions, the Ottoman state demonstrated a remarkable capacity to harness market dynamics for fiscal administration, ensuring resilience and longevity in a rapidly evolving geopolitical landscape.

A significant issue that warrants examination is the Ottoman Empire's inability to transition to a bureaucratic hierarchical order, as observed in other European states (Coşgel and Miceli 2009). Although a partial transition occurred in the eighteenth century, this transformation did not fully manifest until the eighteenth century. The question arises as to why fully hierarchical forms did not emerge earlier in the Ottoman Empire. Edgar Kiser's analysis of early modern tax systems provides a valuable framework for understanding the absence of fully hierarchical forms of tax-farming governance in the Ottoman Empire. Several interrelated factors explain this phenomenon.

The first is the administrative constraint of the empire. The Ottoman Empire's vast territorial expanse and diverse population presented significant administrative challenges. Establishing a robust bureaucratic infrastructure capable of overseeing hierarchical tax collection across such a heterogeneous empire would have required extensive resources and institutional development. Instead, the state relied on hybrid mechanisms such as lifetime contracts to delegate tax-collection tasks, minimizing the need for direct state oversight while leveraging local expertise. Furthermore, the Ottoman administrative system relied heavily on local intermediaries and elites, making centralized hierarchical governance less feasible.

Granting local actors' autonomy through tax-farming contracts helped maintain political stability and minimized the risk of rebellion or resistance. A shift toward fully hierarchical forms might have disrupted these established power dynamics, potentially alienating influential stakeholders and undermining the state's authority.

The second reason is permanent fiscal pressure. The Ottoman Empire's fiscal priorities often necessitated immediate revenue generation, particularly during periods of military conflict or economic strain. The auction-based system provided a prompt and reliable influx of funds, whereas fully hierarchical allocation required long-term investments in administrative capacity and oversight. The third reason can be attributed to the institutional path dependence. Once established, market-oriented systems such as *Iltizam* created institutional path dependencies that made the transition to fully hierarchical forms more challenging. The state's reliance on these systems, coupled with their immediate fiscal advantages, reinforced their persistence, despite their limitations.

The interplay between market and hierarchical forms of tax farming has significant implications for the Ottoman fiscal system and governance. The competitive tax-farming contracts ensured immediate revenue maximization, which was critical during periods of military conflict or economic strain. However, its short-term focus often compromises the tax base's long-term sustainability. The lifetime contracts emphasize long-term revenue stability, reflecting the state's shift toward fiscal consolidation and administrative centralization. The reliance on market mechanisms in the tax-farming contracts highlighted the Ottoman state's limited administrative capacity as competitive bidding reduced the need for direct oversight. The lifetime contracts marked an effort to strengthen bureaucratic control and institutionalize governance, reflecting the evolving administrative priorities of the state. The short-term focus of the tax-farming contracts frequently led to economic distortions, as tax farmers prioritized immediate extraction over sustainable practices. This in turn created social unrest and weakened the state's legitimacy. The lifetime contracts mitigated these effects by promoting stability and incentivizing long-term investments in the tax base. However, the hierarchical allocation process also risked entrenching elite privileges and reducing the state's flexibility in responding to changing economic conditions.

In conclusion, the Ottoman Empire's approach to tax farming illustrates the complex interplay between market and hierarchical forms of governance. The transition from a competitive tax-farming contracts to lifetime contracts reflects the state's efforts to balance immediate revenue needs with long-term administrative control and stability. By examining the dynamics of these systems through the lens of market and hierarchical forms, we gain a deeper understanding of the institutional logic that shaped the Ottoman fiscal system and its broader implications for governance, economic development, and state-society relations. This analysis underscores the adaptability and pragmatism of the Ottoman state in navigating the challenges of revenue collection in the complex and dynamic empire.

A Brief Comparison of Tax Farming in the Ottoman Empire and European States

Tax farming, a prominent fiscal institution in the early modern period, was widely adopted across the Ottoman Empire and European states, albeit with significant variation. This chapter examines the similarities and differences in tax-farming practices between the Ottoman Empire and selected European states through the lens of principal-agent models. Drawing on various scholarly analyses, the discussion focuses on institutional frameworks, the balance between market and hierarchical forms, and the implications of these practices for state capacity and economic performance.

As posited in the preceding sections, the principal-agent model provides a valuable framework for analyzing tax-farming systems. In this context, the state (principal) delegates the task of tax collection to agents (tax farmers) in exchange for fixed payments or revenue share. The model elucidates key dynamics such as information asymmetries, incentive alignment, and the costs of monitoring and enforcement. Market forms, characterized by competitive bidding, prioritize efficiency and immediate revenue maximization, whereas hierarchical forms emphasize bureaucratic control and long-term stability. The balance between these forms reflects the state's administrative capacity, fiscal priorities, and broader institutional arrangements.

The Ottoman Empire implemented a hybrid approach to tax farming by incorporating both market-oriented and hierarchical elements. The tax-farming contract, prevalent during the classical period, exemplifies market-oriented tax farming. The contracts were auctioned to the highest bidder to ensure immediate fiscal gains. Tax farmers were granted significant autonomy, but were incentivized to maximize revenue extraction, often at the expense of social and economic stability. The transition to the lifetime contracts in the late seventeenth century marked a shift toward a more hierarchical approach. Lifetime contracts, allocated through auctions, emphasized stability, and incentivized investment in the tax base. While this system mitigated some of the excesses of short-term contracts, it retained a market component and faced challenges such as favoritism and elite entrenchment.

Under the early Stuarts, tax farming in England relied heavily on market mechanisms (Ashton 1956). Revenue farms are allocated through competitive bidding to ensure fiscal efficiency. However, this approach has been criticized for fostering opportunism and inefficiency. By the late seventeenth century, England transitioned to direct bureaucratic administration, reflecting an increase in state capacity and preference for hierarchical forms. French tax farming, particularly under the ancien régime, combined market, and hierarchical elements. The evolution of revenue farms, from competitive auctions to semi-institutionalized arrangements dominated by powerful financiers, facilitated fiscal stability but often entrenched elite privileges and reduced system flexibility. The inefficiencies of French revenue farms contributed to fiscal crises. Habsburg Spain's reliance on tax farming to finance frequent military campaigns heavily emphasized competitive auctions. However, the focus on short-term revenue often undermines economic sustainability and contributes to serial default. By contrast, Prussian tax farming emphasizes long-term contracts and centralized oversight, aligning with hierarchical principles (Kiser and Schneider 1994). This approach enhanced revenue stability but required significant investments in state infrastructure. The emphasis on bureaucratic allocation reflects the state's strong administrative capacity.

The Ottoman Empire's utilization of market-oriented systems, such as short-term tax-farming contracts aligns with the practices in France and Spain, where competitive auctions predominate (Bonney 1979; Çizakça 1993; Johnson 2006; Drelichman and Voth 2011). In contrast, England's semi-institutionalized revenue farms and Prussia's bureaucratic allocation reflect a greater emphasis on hierarchical structures (Kiser 1987, 1994; Kiser and Schneider 1994; Coşgel and Miceli 2009). These disparities can be attributed to variations in administrative capacity, fiscal priority, and institutional legacy. The Ottoman Empire's vast and diverse territory necessitated decentralized approaches, rendering market forms such as auctions more practical (Salzmann 1993). Conversely, states like Prussia, with a smaller and more homogeneous population, could invest in centralized bureaucratic oversight. States experiencing fiscal strain, such as the Ottoman Empire, France, and Spain, prioritized market mechanisms to secure immediate revenue. In contrast, England and Prussia placed greater emphasis on long-term stability, as evidenced by their hierarchical arrangements. Historical legacies have influenced the evolution of tax-farming systems. The Ottoman Empire's reliance on local elites and intermediaries reinforced the persistence of market-oriented approaches, whereas administrative reforms in England and Prussia facilitated the transition to hierarchical structures.

The Ottoman Empire's predominant utilization of market mechanisms and auctions in the allocation of tax-farming contracts can be attributed to several interconnected factors. The Empire's extensive territorial expanse and administrative complexity rendered centralized oversight of tax-collection impractical. Auctions enabled the state to delegate tax-collection responsibilities to local intermediaries who possessed a superior knowledge of local conditions. This decentralized approach mitigated the administrative burden on the central government, while ensuring revenue inflow. The Ottoman state's frequent military campaigns and infrastructure projects necessitated immediate and predictable revenue stream. Market mechanisms such as competitive auctions provide a means for securing lump-sum payments upfront, addressing the state's short-term fiscal requirements. These auctions allowed the state to transfer the risks and uncertainties of the tax collection to private entities. The auction system enabled the Ottoman state to adapt to the changing economic and political conditions. Through the periodic auctioning of tax farms, the state can adjust contract terms and ensure competition among bidders. This flexibility also facilitated the state's response to regional variations in economic productivity and tax base stability. The reliance on market mechanisms facilitated the integration of local elites into the fiscal system. By granting tax-farming contracts to influential local actors, the state reduced the likelihood of resistance and co-opted these elites to support imperial authority. Auctions provided a transparent and competitive framework that legitimized the allocation of fiscal privileges. Market-oriented tax farming incentivized private actors to maximize revenue collection. Although this often resulted in overextraction and social unrest, it also ensured high initial bids and immediate fiscal gains for the state. The competitive nature of auctions encourages efficiency among bidders who seek to outcompete rivals by demonstrating their revenue-generating potential.

The emergence of bureaucratic forms in England and France during the eighteenth century can be attributed to their evolving administrative capacity, institutional development, and fiscal priorities. Several factors have facilitated the transition from market-based tax farming to direct bureaucratic administration. Both England and France experienced significant advancements in administrative centralization during the seventeenth and eighteenth centuries. In England, the Glorious Revolution of 1688 and subsequent reforms strengthened parliamentary oversight and centralized fiscal control (North and Weingast 1989). In France, the monarchy's efforts to consolidate power led to the establishment of more direct tax-collection mechanisms. The growth of state capacity, including the professionalization of civil service, played a crucial role in the emergence of bureaucratic forms. In England, the establishment of institutions such as the Treasury and Customs and Excise Departments marked a shift toward professional salaried officials handling tax collection. France witnessed similar developments, particularly under the reforms initiated by Colbert (Johnson 2006).

The transition to bureaucratic forms was driven by the necessity of a stable and predictable revenue stream. Market-based systems, which are efficient in the short term, are frequently opportunistic or inefficient. Direct administration enabled these states to streamline tax collection, reduce dependence on intermediaries, and minimize revenue leakage. Institutional reforms in both states established the foundation for bureaucratic administration. England's transition to constitutional monarchy provided a framework for enhanced transparency and accountability in fiscal matters. In France, the shift from tax farming to bureaucratic administration reflects the monarchy's efforts to diminish the influence of financiers and to regain control over fiscal policy. The economic and social transformations of the eighteenth century, including the emergence of capitalist economies and expanding state functions, necessitated more efficient and centralized tax systems. Bureaucratic forms allow states to adapt to these changes and manage growing fiscal demand more effectively.

The choice between the market and hierarchical forms has significant implications for state capacity and economic performance. Market mechanisms such as auctions ensure immediate revenue maximization but often result in overextraction and social unrest. Hierarchical forms promote long-term stability but require greater investments in administrative infrastructure. Market-oriented systems allowed states like the Ottoman Empire to adapt to changing conditions, while hierarchical forms such as Prussia enhanced control and predictability. The reliance on local elites in market systems mitigated resistance but increased elite entrenchment. Hierarchical forms fostered greater state control but occasionally alienated regional actors.

The comparative study of tax farming in the Ottoman Empire and European states highlights the complex interplay between market and hierarchical forms in shaping fiscal institutions. While the Ottoman Empire's reliance on market mechanisms reflects its administrative constraints and fiscal priorities, European states, such as Prussia and France, illustrate the potential of hierarchical arrangements to enhance state capacity. By examining these systems through the lens of principal-agent models, this analysis contributes to our understanding of the institutional foundations of early modern states and their long-term trajectories.

Assessment of the Study, Its Potential Contributions, and Suggestions for Future Research

This study addresses critical questions pertaining to the development of welfare-enhancing institutions from a theoretical perspective, focusing on the Ottoman Empire's tax-collection institutions in the early modern period. By examining the conditions that facilitate the development of resilient and welfare-promoting institutions in certain societies, this study makes a significant contribution to our understanding of how state structures and policies influence long-term societal outcomes. The comparative approach employed in this study, which contrasts the Ottoman Empire with Western Europe and China, offers valuable insights into broader global patterns of institutional development. The theoretical framework-based analyses, assumptions, and propositions presented in this study necessitate a more comprehensive examination through empirical and qualitative studies utilizing historical data. Incorporating historical approaches may facilitate the resolution of specific questions and problems.

This study contributes to the existing literature on institutional development by incorporating principal-agent models and contracting approaches to assess how commitment problems and governance structures affected tax collection in the early modern Ottoman Empire. The focus on institutional dynamics within a non-Western context enriches comparative studies of political economy and highlights the unique challenges faced by the Ottomans, offering an alternative perspective to the Eurocentric narratives that predominate in institutional theory. Moreover, the study critically examines the institutional mechanisms that led to persistent weaknesses in the Ottoman Empire's tax-collection systems and compares these mechanisms with those of Western Europe. This comparison contributes to our understanding of how institutional design can facilitate or impede the development of effective welfare-enhancing policies.

On the other hand, the emergence of tax-farming contracts and a market-based system based on auctions in the Ottoman Empire was necessary and important for the most effective results. It was costlier for an empire to spread over a large geography to create hierarchical and bureaucratic forms like European states with smaller borders (Salzmann 1993, 2004). Furthermore, instead of transferring tax revenues directly to the central treasury, the Ottoman Empire also allowed taxes to be spent in the regions in which they were collected, thus ensuring that a certain monetary base remained in circulation (İnalcık 2000, p. 104). In this way, especially in the eighteenth century, when lifetime contracts were intense, both the number of contracts increased by 209 percent and the income obtained from these contracts increased by approximately 88 percent (Çizakça 1989, p. 67).

The central theme in this study revolves around the paradoxical issue of why certain societies, such as those in Western Europe, succeeded in developing welfare-enhancing institutions, whereas others, including the Ottoman Empire, faced persistent institutional weaknesses. Why did the Ottoman Empire experience difficulties establishing welfare-enhancing institutions despite its vast territorial reach and economic resources? How did alterations in tax-collection systems in the Ottoman Empire reflect broader shifts in political and economic structures, and what implications did these shifts have on the empire's institutional resilience? What were the structural differences between the Ottoman Empire's tax systems and those in Western Europe and China and how did these differences contribute to divergent institutional outcomes? These questions are crucial for understanding the broader dynamics of institutional failure and success and to elucidate the mechanisms behind the development or stagnation of public welfare systems. By addressing these questions, this study contributes to the broader field of comparative political economy and offers insights into the historical and institutional factors that determine the efficacy and inadequacy of welfare systems.

Future research can extend this analysis by exploring several key areas. While this study focuses on the Ottoman Empire, expanding its comparative scope to include other regions of the Islamic world and non-Western societies could offer a more comprehensive understanding of institutional development. Further examination of regions such as Safavid Persia, Mughal India, and East Asia could elucidate how different political and economic structures interact with tax policies and welfare systems. A longitudinal study that traces the development of tax-collection systems and their impact on welfare over an extended period in the Ottoman Empire could provide more detailed insights into the long-term effects of institutional design. This would facilitate a more robust comparison of the short- and long-term outcomes of tax policies, and their implications for state stability and public welfare. Given the long-term consequences of early modern institutions on contemporary governance structures, future research could also investigate how the institutional legacies of the Ottoman Empire, particularly in terms of welfare systems and tax collection, continued to influence the modern Middle Eastern and Eastern European states. Another avenue for future research could involve examining the role of non-state actors such as merchant guilds or religious institutions in shaping the tax-collection process and welfare systems. Understanding the interplay between state and non-state actors in the provision of public goods and services could offer additional insights into the institutional dynamics of this period. By expanding the scope of inquiry to encompass these domains, subsequent investigations could further elucidate the intricacies inherent in welfare-enhancing institutions, and facilitate more comprehensive comparative analyses between diverse historical and geographical contexts.

Conclusion

This study explored the challenges and complexities surrounding the development of tax-farming institutions from a theoretical perspective, with a focus on the Ottoman Empire's tax-collection systems during the early modern period. By adopting a comparative approach, this study elucidates the significant differences between the Ottoman Empire and Western Europe in their capacity to establish and maintain institutions that promote welfare and stability.

These findings underscore the critical role of institutional design and governance structures in shaping the state development trajectory. While the Ottoman Empire possessed the economic resources and territorial expanse necessary to develop effective welfare systems, persistent structural weaknesses in its tax-collection mechanisms coupled with broader political and economic constraints impeded the establishment of such institutions. The study demonstrates how these institutional challenges, particularly related to commitment problems and governance inefficiencies, differentiated the Ottoman Empire from its Western European counterparts, who were better positioned to innovate and develop systems conducive to welfare enhancement. Furthermore, this study contributes to the broader field of comparative political economy by providing an in-depth analysis of the Ottoman Empire's institutional landscape and juxtaposing it with other global powers during this period. This perspective offers novel insights into the global patterns of institutional development and the factors that enabled some societies to successfully construct resilient and effective welfare systems, whereas others, such as the Ottomans, grappled with institutional stagnation.

The conclusions of this study provide a foundation for future research, particularly by expanding the geographic scope of comparative studies, investigating the long-term implications of Ottoman institutions, and examining the role of non-state actors in shaping welfare systems. By extending the analysis to these areas, researchers can enhance their understanding of the dynamics that influence the establishment and sustainability of welfare-enhancing institutions not only in the context of the Ottoman Empire but also across diverse historical and geographical contexts. Ultimately, this study contributes to our understanding of the complex interplay between political, economic, and institutional factors that shape the development of state capacity and public welfare systems. This underscores the significance of institutional design in determining the long-term resilience and effectiveness of state policies, offering valuable insights into both historical inquiry and contemporary governance.

Some questions raised in this concise review are based on this theoretical perspective, and the historical data related to these questions are presented in the subsequent chapters of this book. Although these chapters cannot address all approaches, assumptions, and questions based on this theoretical framework, they provide a partial contribution. These theoretical questions are addressed not only through the analysis of contractual relations, but also through historical approaches based on the centralization of the legal structure and specific Ottoman tax farmers who played a significant role in these contracts.

References

Abou-El-Haj, R. A. (2000). *Modern Devletin Doğası: 16. Yüzyıldan 18. Yüzyıla Osmanlı İmparatorluğu* (translated by Oktay Özel and Canay Şahin). İmge Kitabevi.

Altay, B. and Oğuz, F. (2021). *Rules, Contracts and Law Enforcement in the Ottoman Empire: The Case of Tax-Farming Contracts*. Palgrave Macmillan.

Ashton, R. (1956). Revenue Farming under the Early Stuarts. *The Economic History Review* 8(3), 310–322.

Balla, E. and Johnson, N. D. (2009). Fiscal Crisis and Institutional Change in the Ottoman Empire and France. *The Journal of Economic History* 69(3), 809–845.

Bonney, R. J. (1979). The Failure of French Revenue Farms, 1600–60. *The Economic History Review* 32(1), 11–32.

Çizakça, M. (1989). Tax-Farming and Resource Allocation in Past Islamic Societies. *Journal of King Abdulaziz University: Islamic Economics* 1, 59–80.

Çizakça, M. (1993). Tax-Farming and Financial Decentralization in the Ottoman Empire, 1520–1697. *The Journal of European Economic History* 22, 219–250.

Çizakça, M. (1996). *Comparative Evolution of Business Partnerships: The Islamic World and Europe, with Special Reference to the Ottoman Archives*. Brill.

Coşgel, M. and Miceli, T. (2009). Tax Collection in History. *Public Finance Review* 37, 399–420.

Darling, L. (1996). *Revenue-Rising and Legitimacy: Tax Collection and Finance Administration in the Ottoman Empire, 1560–1660*. Leiden: Brill.

Drelichman, M. and Voth, H. (2011). Serial Defaults, Serial Profits: Returns to Sovereign Lending in Habsburg Spain, 1566–1600. *Explorations in Economic History* 48, 1–19.

Genç, M. (2000). *Osmanlı İmparatorluğu'nda Devlet ve Ekonomi*. Ötüken.

İnalcık, H. (2000). *Osmanlı İmparatorluğu'nun Sosyal ve Ekonomik Tarihi I*. Eren.

İnalcık, H. (2017). *The Ottoman Empire and Europe: The Ottoman Empire and its Place in European History*. Kronik.

Johnson, N. D. (2006). Banking on the King: The Evolution of the Royal Revenue Farms in Old Regime France. *The Journal of Economic History*, 66(4), 963–991.

Johnson, N. D. and Koyama, M. (2014). Tax Farming and the Origins of State Capacity in England and France. *Explorations in Economic History* 51, 1–20.
Johnson, N. D. and Koyama, M. (2017). States and Economic Growth: Capacity and Constraints. *Explorations in Economic History* 64, 1–20.
Karaman, K. (2009). Decentralized Coercion and Self-Restrain in Provincial Taxation: The Ottoman Empire 15th–16th Centuries. *Journal of Economic Behavior and Organization* 71, 690–703.
Karaman, K. and Pamuk, Ş. (2010). Ottoman State Finance in European Perspective, 1500–1914. *The Journal of Economic History* 70, 593–629.
Kiser, E. (1987). The Formation of State Policy in Western European Absolutism: A Comparison of England and France. *Politics & Society*, 15, 259–315.
Kiser, E. (1994). Markets and Hierarchies in Early Modern Tax Systems: A Principal-Agent Analysis. *Politics and Society*, 22, 284–315.
Kiser, E. and Kane, J. (2001). Revolution and State Structure: The Bureaucratization of Tax Administration in Early Modern England and France. *American Journal of Sociology* 107, 183–223.
Kiser, E. and Linton, A. (2001). Determinants of the Growth of the State: War and Taxation in Early Modern France and England. *Social Forces* 80, 411–448.
Kiser, E. and Schneider, J. (1994). Bureaucracy and Efficiency: An Analysis of Taxation in Early Modern Prussia. *American Sociological Review* 59, 187–204.
Ma, D. and Rubin, J. (2019). The Paradox of Power: Principal-Agent Problems and Administrative Capacity in Imperial China (and Other Absolutist Regimes). *Journal of Comparative Economics* 47, 277–294.
North, D. and Weingast, B. (1989). Constitutions and Commitment: The Evolution of Institutions Governing Public Choice in Seventeenth-Century England. *The Journal of Economic History* 49, 803–832.
Pamuk, Ş. (2000). The Ottoman Empire in the Eighteenth Century. *Itinerario* 24, 104–116.
Pamuk, Ş. (2004a). The Evolution of Financial Institutions in the Ottoman Empire, 1600–1914. *Financial History Review* 11, 7–32.
Pamuk, Ş. (2004b). Institutional Change and the Longevity of the Ottoman Empire, 1500–1800. *The Journal of Interdisciplinary History* 35, 225–247.
Salzmann, A. (1993). An Ancien Regime Revisited: "Privatization" and Political Economy in the Eighteenth-Century Ottoman Empire. *Politics and Society* 21, 393–423.
Salzmann, A. (2004). *Tocqueville in the Ottoman Empire: Rival Paths to the Modern State*. Brill.
Tezcan, B. (2010). *Second Ottoman Empire: Political and Social Transformation in the Early Modern World*. Cambridge University Press.

White, E. (2004). From Privatized to Government-Administrated Tax Collection: Tax Farming in Eighteenth Century France. *The Economic History Review* 57, 636–663.

Yaycıoğlu, A. (2016). *Partners of the Empire: The Crisis of the Ottoman Order in the Age of Revolutions*. Stanford University Press.

CHAPTER 4

A Research on Tax-Farming (Iltizam) Contracts in the Ottoman Empire: The Case of Bolu

Ümit Katırancı

Introduction

From the second half of the sixteenth century onward, a series of changes took place in the political, administrative, financial, and social structure of the Ottoman Empire. A number of events such as the increasing importance of salaried armies equipped with firearms as a result of advances in war technology, the price revolution caused by American silver and gold, population growth in the sixteenth century, the climate crisis, the Jalali rebellions in Anatolia, and the expansion of the bureaucracy prompted the state to take measures (İnalcık 1980; Faroqhi 1994; Darling 1996). In the face of these circumstances, Ottoman rulers attempted to use some

Ü. Katırancı (✉)
Faculty of Science and Letter, Ankara Haci Bayram Veli University, Ankara, Turkey
e-mail: umit.katiranci@hbv.edu.tr

B. Altay (ed.), *Revenue-Raising Institutions, State Organization and Economic Change in the Early Modern Ottoman Empire*, Palgrave Studies in Economic History,
https://doi.org/10.1007/978-3-031-96492-3_4

methods to transfer provincial revenues to the central treasury and to meet the state's need for cash. In one hand, the state regularly demanded levies collected in extraordinary situations to directly entered into the state treasury. These extraordinary levies, which is called *avariz*, *imdadiye*, and *tekalif*, were regularized in cash or in kind (İnalcık 1980, pp. 313–327). On the other hand, the *iltizam* (tax-farming) system, also which is the main subject of this study, became widespread throughout the empire (Pamuk 2021, pp. 146–148).

Iltizam means contracting out the right to collecting any revenue, income, or taxes belonging to the state to a private entrepreneur for a limited period, usually up to 3 years. The private bidders are referred to in the archival documents under the name of *mültezim* or *âmil/ameldâr* (Genç 2022, p. 107; Baer 1986, p. 1154; İnalcık 1980, p. 327). The *mültezim* could be a person or a partnership (Darling 1996, pp. 129–130). If the revenue source, each mukātaʿa, is collected by state officials, this procedure is called *emânet*, and the official who manages it is called *emîn*. The emīn was appointed directly by the treasury and awarded as timar or a salary (Tabakoğlu 2020, p. 338).

The state revenue sources in the iltizam system are called mukātaʿa, which means subdivision. In its broader sense, the term mukātaʿa is a financial unit that state revenue sources is divided into portions to be distributed in return for a mutually agreed-upon price (Darling 1996, p. 123). A mukātaʿa could include all kinds of revenue source within the Ottoman economy. mukātaʿa dates to the Abbasid period and has been used in the Ottoman Empire since early times. While the mukātaʿa term initially meant the assignment of revenues to iltizam in return for a certain amount, in time, it gained the meaning of a tax unit underlying the system (Genç 2022, pp. 97–98; Tabakoğlu 2020, p. 327).

The main purpose of the iltizam system was the most efficient delivery of state revenues to the treasury and the rapid cash flow to the treasury. So, the auction method was adopted. Bidders undertake to pay a certain amount to the state to obtain the mukātaʿa. The highest bidder wins the right to collect taxes. Since the amount to be paid to the state is certain here, there is no loss of income on behalf of the state. The responsibility and risk associated with tax collection are shifted from the government to the tax farmer. This individual not only undertakes the labor involved in the collection process but is also obligated, frequently in advance, to provide the entire amount stipulated in the contract, regardless of whether the revenue source proves to be productive (Darling 1996, p. 119). For the tax farmer, it tries to eliminate the financial burden created by the amount to be paid to the state in advance by collecting taxes. If he collects more revenue than the amount he had promised, he can make a high profit (Darling 1996, pp. 119–120). As for the *emîns*, they were not affected by the lack of revenue from the tax unit or its loss. Especially state revenues that did not attract refugees and important sources of income such as state-owned lands, mines, and customs were managed by the eminent persons.

In the iltizam system, mukātaʿa were usually auctioned for term of one to three years, called *tahvil*. The rationale for this was to consider the optimal conditions of the mukātaʿa. This is because a mukātaʿa might not have the same favorable conditions for every year. Moreover, in the system, if someone increased the price of the mukātaʿa before the expiry of the three-year period, it could be auctioned to the higher bidder, provided that the right of priority was reserved for the current tax farmer. Here, it is important that the former tax farmer does not accept the new bid price. Because, due to this offer, the tahvil may be transferred to someone else without waiting for the expiry of its term. On the other hand, toward the end of the term of the tahvil, the tahvil may be merged by re-introducing the mukātaʿa which he had been operating with a new bid (Tabakoğlu 2020, pp. 331–332).

The highest bidder would be obliged to pay a certain payment in advance in return for granting the mukātaʿa in accordance with the terms of the contract. Afterward, he continued to pay in monthly, quarterly, or semi-annual installments. Therefore, the tax farmers make a significant contribution to the financing of state expenditures through the cash advance and installments they pay to the state. On the other hand, they contributed with the goods or services they produced in the mukātaʿas. The new position of the state with iltizam became the controller of the producer rather than the producer. Thus, the relationship between the state, the actual owner of the revenue, and the tax farmer (mültezim), the operator of the revenue, was in favor of the state, which had the right to intervene. The state had the right to terminate the contract whenever it pleased (İnalcık 1980, p. 328; Tabakoğlu 2020, p. 332; Genç 2022, p. 108).

The process of iltizam took place through various stages. The bidder(s) bidding for a mukātaʿa applied with a petition (arzuhal) to the *kâdî* of the region where the mukātaʿa was located or to the leading financial officials (defterdar, muhassil, etc.). In the application, the amount offered for the mukāta^ca, the amount of down payment to be paid, bidder's conditions, if any, the list of guarantors and the amounts committed by the guarantors (*kefil*) are written. The highest bidder was inspected by the kâdî. The kâdî personally inspects whether the bidder is able to perform the taxation properly, whether he is able to pay the amount he has offered, and whether his kefils are able to pay the amount they have pledged. He then sends the bidder's offer to the center. If it is accepted, tax-farming contract is prepared by the state and sended a berât with the content of the offer to the bidder and the state's demands, if any. When the bidder received this berât, he started tax farming (Genç 2022, p. 108; Darling 1996, pp. 133–134; Çakır 2003, pp. 146–147).

As a result of the granting of the mukātaᶜa, two procedures were applied when making payments. The first of these is *kıste'l-yevm*. This is the daily collection value that emerges by dividing the price of iltizam by the number of days of saving. The tax farmer paid installments to the state based on the *kıste'l-yevm*, or when the mukātaᶜa changed hands, the remaining days of the refugee were calculated and accounted for in this way. With this accounting method, the amount is transferred to the Treasury (Genç 2022, p. 108; Tabakoğlu 2020, p. 333). The other is the annual calculation based on the receipts called *(makbûz)*. This method was generally applied to mukātaᶜa collected by the *emânet*. *Emin* records the revenues collected within a year, submits them to the approval of the kâdî and delivers them to the state. (Çakır 2003, pp. 68, 117).

In the iltizam system, there were many officials with various functions, and they were interconnected with each other. *Nâzir* was responsible for protecting the income associated with an iltizam as its chief overseer. The nazirs could be chosen by the choice of the mültezims or by way of iltizam or kefâlet. The main duties of the nazirs were to account the mukātaᶜa revenues and check their accuracy and to forward the iltizam contracts to the center together with the *müfettiş*es (Darling 1996, p. 131; Çakır 2003, pp. 124–125). Sometimes a hierarchical structure could emerge among the nazirs. In this case, *nâzir-i nüzzâr*, who was usually the local high-ranking administrator (sancakbeyi, beylerbeyi, etc.), was placed above the nâzirs (Çakır 2003, p. 127; Darling 1996, p. 131).

The inspector (*müfettiş*) and the kâdî had an important role in supervision of iltizams. Inspectors were usually preferred from among the kâdîs. A kâdî could be the inspector of mukātaᶜa in another region. They could be responsible for a province or a region. It was one of his duties to inspect the iltizams and to assign them to trustworthy, whealty, and capable of tax-farming bidders who were in good financial condition and capable of collecting taxes. They were also kept an accounting of *emins*, *âmils*, or *mültezims*. The inspectors were also responsible for collecting the remaining sums of the mültezims at the end of the tahvil and disconnecting with the mukāta^cas. (MAD.4689, p. 59). The kâdîs were also the financial officers. All kinds of legal problems in the mukāta^cas directly concerned them. They reported any irregularities to the center (Darling 1996, p. 131) (Çakır 2003, pp. 132–136).

There were also other officials who assisted the mültezim or emin. One of these was *kâbız-i mâl*. Subordinate to the mültezim, kâbız-i mâl collected the revenues of the mukāta^cas. He was as responsible for the payments to be made to the state as the mültezim (Darling 1996, p. 130; Çakır 2003, pp. 136–137). A nazir, an emin, or any guarantor (kefil) could be the kâbız-i mâl. Also, there was a scribe (kâtip) who kept the accounts of the mültezim/emin and prepared the financial reports of the mukāta^cas. There was also a person named *havale*, who was in charge of delivering the expenditures made from the mukāta^ca revenues to the allocated fonds. Finally, the prohibitionists *(yasakçı)*, who checked whether the rules of the mukāta^ca were being followed, was another personnel of the mültezim. Preventing interventions in the mukāta^ca and collecting the fines imposed on those living in the mukāta^ca were also among the duties of them (Çakır 2003, p. 140). From the seventeenth century onward, prohibitors were not seen in mukāta^cas (Darling 1996, p. 131).

At the end of the term of the tahvil, the mültezim might have incurred losses or become bankrupt because of extraordinary circumstances. If mültezim had not stipulated a special condition for such a situation in the contract, his property could be confiscated since all his assets were mortgaged to the treasury. However, since the kefils and guarantee fees are written in the contract, the amount due to the treasury is collected from them (Darling 1996, p. 131; Çakır 2003, pp. 143–145; Tabakoğlu 2020, p. 333).

In order to provide an example of the tax-farming (iltizam) system in the provinces, this study examines the tax farm contracts of the mukāta^ca in Bolu sanjak in Anatolia. The time span of the study covers the period from the late sixteenth century to the second quarter of the seventeenth century, the period when the tax farming began to spread. The main purpose of the study is to provide a regional-based analysis of the tax-farming system. The mukāta^ca, bidders, personnel, and especially the bidder's conditions in the contracts will be evaluated in the study. Thus, one of the focal points of this study is to contribute to what is known about the tax farming in the age of crisis and change by adding new information by presenting local-based research.

Tax-Farming Contracts of Mukātaᶜas of Bolu

As mukātaᶜa were revenue sources, these were hierarchically linked to the central treasury. There are mukātaᶜa bureaus (kalemler) under the central treasury. These were as follows: *Muhasebe-i Evvel (Başmuhasebe), Jizye Muhasebesi, Ziyade-i Jizye, Harameyn Muhasebesi, Harameyn Mukātaᶜa, Mevkufat, Mukātaᶜa-i Evvel (Başmukātaᶜa), Maden Mukātaᶜa, Haslar Mukātaᶜa, Hâssha-i Cedide, Bursa Mukātaᶜa, Mensuhat, Istanbul Mukātaᶜa, Avlonya Mukātaᶜa, Ağriboz Mukātaᶜa, Cedide-i Ulâ, Cedide-i Sânî, Kefe Mukātaᶜa, Agnam-i Celebkeşan (Ganem Mukātaᶜa), Anatolian Accounting and Bishop (Şıkk-i Sânî/Maliye) Mukātaᶜa.*

The Bureau of Bursa Mukātaᶜas was responsible for the accounts of Bursa, Biga, Balıkesir, Bolu, Adapazarı, Kastamonu, Sinop, Çankırı, Kocaeli, the islands in the Mediterranean and the mizan-i harir (silk trap) mukātaᶜa. (Çakır 2003, p. 105; Tabakoğlu 2020, p. 285). Bolu was attached to the Bursa Mukātaᶜa Bureau as a *nezâret* (supervision) (MAD.d 5254, p. 2). Therefore, the iltizam records and accounts of Bolu are also included in the records of this fund (D.BRM). Also, *Maliyeden Müdevver* fonds provides iltizam contracts about Bolu. The defters in this fund containing the iltizam contracts identified for the period in question to be used in this study and their dates are as follows (Table 4.1):

The nazirs held the Supervision (Nezaret) of Bolu Mukâtaᶜas by way of undertaking (ber-vech-i iltizam). For this reason, they are referred to as *nâzir-i mültezim* in the sources (MAD.4689, p. 28). In line with the general trend of the period, all the nazirs (except for unidentified one)

Table 4.1 Sources

Register Nr	*Date*
MAD.d 4689	1596–1602
MAD.d 5452	1602–1617
MAD.d 1842	1610–1614
MAD.d 1850	1611–1614
MAD.d 7299	1616–1626
MAD.d 3305	1624–1626

comes from the military class. 6 nazirs in Bolu are mentioned in the documents of the period under study. While the identity of one of them is unknown, four of them were *çavuş*. The most prominent one in terms of rank is Mustafa Bey, the former bookkeeper (defterdâr) of Erzurum. The nâzirs in Bolu generally completed their three-year terms. Bids for the nâzirs came toward the end of the tahvil. From this, the iltizam of the Bolu nezaret seems to have been consistent and stable with the duration of the tahvil. The table below shows the ministers of the Bolu mukata (Table 4.2):

The number of mukāta^cas controlled by the nazirs in charge of Mukāta^cas of Bolu is 12. In the contract of the Bolu Nezâret dated 1600, 10 mukāta^cas names are recorded (MAD.4689, p. 28). However, in later records, this number increased to 12 with the mukāta^ca not included in this list of Mukāta^ca (MAD.1842, p. 18; MAD.4689, p. 57). These mukāta^cas consists of a wide variety of revenues. These were revenues from estates and villages, as well as revenues from the pier customs, rice, saffron, mills, dyehouses, ihtisab (market) and ihzariye (court fees), jizya, and awqaf revenues. The mukāta^ca at the disposal of the nâzir of Bolu are as follows (Table 4.3):

The *müfettiş*es in Bolu were usually those whom the nâzirs wished in accordance with the terms of the contract. For example, Bayram Çavuş, the nazir of Bolu, wanted to appoint a kâdî of his choice as a müfettiş (MAD.4689, p. 28). The kâdîs who became müfettiş were usually the kâdîs of the sanjak or its dependent districts. This is more clearly seen in the case of Bolu. The müfettişes of Bolu were usually the kâdîs of center district or other districts in Bolu. There was not any kâdî of a city outside Bolu as a müfettiş. If they failed to perform their duties properly, they could be dismissed. For example, Bayram was dismissed because he could not fulfill his duty properly and another kadi named Mevlânâ Sururi was appointed in his place (MAD.4658, p. 59). In another example, Fazlullah was dismissed because he and Musa Çavuş and their armed men went from villages collecting extra fees (A.DVN.MHM 82, 87/354). The inspectors identified for Bolu are as follows (Table 4.4):

One of the common practices within the iltizam system is the simultaneous management of more than one mukāta^ca by a single mültezim. This method reduces the number of people the state must deal with in terms of the revenues to be collected. With this method, a bidder bids for more than one mukāta^ca. If he gains the bid, he stipulates in the terms of the contract that the accounts should be kept together and that the surplus

Table 4.2 Mukātaᶜat Nazirs of Bolu

Place	*Date*	*Iltizam period*	*Iltizam bid (akçe)*	*Mültezim*	*Identity*	*Source*
Bolu and Kocaeli	1571	3 years	1.549.000	Hacı Bayram		A.DVN.MHM.d 25 80/898
Bolu and Kocaeli	1574	3 years	1.849.000	Rum Beyoğlu Hüseyin Çavuş	From the çavuşes of Anatolia	A.DVN.MHM.d 25 80/898
Bolu and Kocaeli	1580	–	–	Abdülcelil		A.DVN.MHM.d 41 29/59; 42/87; 76/167
Bolu	1594	3 years	2.700.000	Bayram Çavuş	From the çavuşes of Sultan's court (Dergâh-i Âlî)	AE.SMMD.III 1/4
Bolu	1597	3 years	2.800.339	Bayram Çavuş	From the çavuşes of Sultan's court (Dergâh-i Âlî)	MAD.4689, p. 28
Bolu	1600	3 years	3.100.339	Bayram Çavuş	From the çavuşes of Sultan's court (Dergâh-i Âlî)	MAD.4689, p. 28
Bolu	1603		3.300.339	Mustafa Çavuş b. Mehmed	From the residents of Bolu	MAD.5452, p. 3a
Bolu	1606	6 years	6.661.078	Mustafa Çavuş b. Mehmed	old defterdar of Erzurum	MAD.5452, p. 3a-b
Bolu	1607			Mustafa Bey	Old sancakbeyi	MAD.5452, p. 58a;148a

revenue of one mukātaᶜa should be used for the deficiency of the revenue of the other mukātaᶜa. Thus, with one bid, the mültezim became the tax farmer of several mukātaᶜas. Thus, the mültezim's risk ratio decreases, because if he cannot cover the amount, he has to pay for one mukātaᶜa, he can cover the shortfall from the surplus income of the other one. The

Table 4.3 Mukātaᶜas of Bolu under the control of Nâzirs zirs

	Mukātaᶜas
1	Mukātaᶜa-i Çeltük-i Enhâr-i Konrapa ve Tevâbiᶜha
2	Mukātaᶜa-i Çeltük-i Enhâr-i Kıbrus
3	Mukātaᶜa-i Gümrük-i İskele-i Bendereğli
4	Mukātaᶜa-i Karye-i Çak tâbiᶜ-i Yedidivan ᶜan zeᶜâmet-i Hamza Çelebi re'îsü'l-küttâb
5	Mukātaᶜa-i Hâsshâ-i Hacı Paşa
6	Mukātaᶜa-i Gölvaroş
7	Mukātaᶜa-i Hâsshâ-i İfrâz-i Cedîd
8	Mukātaᶜa-i Karye-i Bedel der kazâ-i Eflânî tâbiᶜ-i Mukâtaᶜa-i Hâsshâ-i Hacı Paşa
9	Mukātaᶜa-i Mevkûfât-i Livâ-i Bolu
10	Mukātaᶜa-i İhtisâb ve İhzâriye-i Nefs-i Bolu ve Karye-i Boyalu ve Tevâbiᶜhâ
11	Mukātaᶜa-i Beytü'l-mâl-i Hâssa-i Liva-i Bolu
12	Mukātaᶜa-i Hâdis-i Resm-i Zağferan ve Resm-i Âsiyabhâ-i Hâdis ve Boyahane-i Taraklıborlu ve Zevaid-i Evkâf-ı Süleyman Paşa

Table 4.4 Mukātaᶜat Müfettişes of Bolu

Müfettiş	*Date*	*Identity*	*Source*
Mevlânâ Zekeriya	1576	Kadi of Mudurnu	A.DVN.MHM.d 28, 358/917
Mevlânâ Abdülcelil	1579	Kadi of Viranşehir	A.DVN.MHM.d 41, 41/85; 76/167
Mevlânâ Nazar	1580	Kadi of Konrapa	A.DVN.MHM.d 41, 455/968
Mevlânâ Muslihuddin	1581		A.DVN.MHM.d 42, 303/929
Mevlânâ Halil	1588	Kadi of Bolu	A.DVN.MHM.d 64, 88/254
Mevlânâ Bayram	1600		MAD.4689, p. 59
Mevlânâ Sururi	1600	Old kadi of Viranşehir	MAD.4689, p. 57
Mevlânâ Ahmed	1604?		MAD.5452, p. 3
Mevlânâ Hibetullah	1605		MAD.5452, p. 3
Mevlânâ İbrahim	1606	Kadi of Taraklıborlu	MAD.5452, p. 99
Mevlânâ Fazlullah	1618		A.DVN.MHM 82, 87/354
Mevlânâ Şaban	1619		MAD.7299, p. 82

worst-case scenario, of course, is that a mültezim is unable to collect the amount he is required to pay under the terms of the contract from both mukātaᶜas in his tahvil.

In Bolu, some mukātaᶜas were auctioned together with several ones. The Çeltik (unshelled rice) revenues produced in the surrounding rivers of Konrapa and Kıbrıs districts in Bolu were usually tendered together (MAD.4689, p. 54). However, the Çeltik of the Konrapa and Cyprus rivers were separate mukātaᶜas, which were as follows: Çeltük-i Enhâr-i Konrapa ve Tevâbiᶜhâ and Çeltük-i Enhâr-i Kıbrus. On the other hand, revenues belonging to the state treasury were also granted in a similar manner. For example, in Bolu, some *hâs*, *mevkûfat,* and *Beytü'l-mâl* revenues were also given in the same way (MAD.1842, p. 18). Here, too, there are three different mukātaᶜa: Hâsshâ-i İfrâz-i Cedid, Mevkûfât-i Livâ-i Bolu, and Beytü'l-mâl-i Hâssa.

The mukātaᶜas that generate the highest revenue under nezâret are the Çeltik mukātaᶜas in Bolu. From this perspective, the most intensive rice cultivation in Bolu is done in Konrapa. In fact, prior to the broad adoption of the iltizam system, it was really the greatest source of income for the sultan in the sanjak. In the Bolu sanjak, the sultan's income in 1530 was 213,200 akçe, of which 158,535 akçe came from Konrapa Çeltik. This amounted to almost 75% of the sultan's revenues coming from the sanjak (Taş 1993, pp. 61–64). It is believed that the mukātaᶜa revenues reached 1,200,000 at the end of the century. The table below displays the costs for this mukātaᶜa (Table 4.5):

The mukātaᶜa had been granted to Halil in 1598. At the end of 3-years tahvil, Mustafa Çavuş, who was the mültezim of Kıbrıs Çeltik mukātaᶜa for 430,000 akçe, also became mültezim the Konrapa Çeltik

Table 4.5 Mukātaᶜa-i Çeltük-i Enhâr-i Konrapa ve Tevâbiᶜhâ

Date (Hijri)	*Date*	*Bid*	*Bidder (Mültezim)*	*Source*
27.01.1007	30.08.1598	1.200.000	Halil	MAD.4689, p. 28
01.02.1010	01.08.1601	1.200.000	Mustafa Çavuş (Emin)	MAD.4689, p. 54
13.03.1013	09.08.1604	1.200.000	Mustafa Çavuş (Emin)	MAD.5452, p. 58
15.03.1013	11.08.1604	1.300.000	Hasan Yarlı	MAD.5452, p. 58

Mukātaᶜa for 1,200,000 akçe, so he took two mukātaᶜas with 1,630,000 akçe. According to the list of kefils of Mustafa Çavuş for the conditions of the contract, 66 people were listed as kefils for 502,000 akçe (MAD.4689, p. 55). There was not any information about the relationship between Mustafa Çavuş and these kefils. Mustafa Çavuş did not deliver the revenues he had collected when tahvil expires. As a result, the Nazir Mustafa Bey, separated the mukātaᶜas of Cyprus and Konrapa and contracted out the Konrapa mukātaᶜa back to Mustafa Çavuş. However, although a year had passed since the bid, Mustafa Çavuş did not send the outstanding taxes and he fled. A soldier named Hasan Yarlı, who had a salary of 13 akçe from the 32nd Troop of the Ulufeciyan-i Yesâr, undertook 2,600,000 akçe for 6 years to the vacant mukātaᶜa (MAD.5452, p. 58). This mukātaᶜa was later added to the royal domains (hâs) (MAD.18131, p. 1) (Table 4.6).

In Kıbrıs, although not as much as in Konrapa, there was still profitable rice production. Sultan's income in 1530 the 213,200 akçe, of which 25,000 akçe came from Kıbrıs Çeltik. This was about 11% of the total income (Taş 1993, pp. 61–64). By the end of the century, this amount had reached 430,000 akçe. Mustafa Çavuş, one of the guards of Sultan's court, undertook iltizam for 430,000 akçe. As mentioned above, the Cyprus Çeltik Mukātaᶜa was given to the tax farm with the Konrapa Çeltik Mukātaᶜa. After Mustafa Çavuş's five-year contract, Hasan Yarlı, the tax farmer of Konrapa, undertook this mukātaᶜa, too. The mukātaᶜa was attached to Royal Domains (Havâss-I Hümâyûn) from the second half of the seventeenth century (AE.SİBR 5/538).

Bolu had four ports due to its coastline on the Black Sea. They were Amasra, Bendereğli, Akçaşehir, and Bartın (Taş 1993, p. 168).

Table 4.6 Mukātaᶜa-i Çeltük-i Enhar-i Kıbrus

Date (Hijri)	*Date*	*Bid*	*Bidder (Mültezim)*	*Source*
27.01.1007	30.08.1598	430.000	Mustafa Çavuş (Emin)	MAD.4689, p. 28
01.02.1010	01.08.1601	430.000	Mustafa Çavuş (Emin)	MAD.4689, p. 54
13.03.1013	09.08.1604	430.000	Mustafa Çavuş (Emin)	MAD.5452, p. 58
15.03.1013	16.03.1613		Hasan Yarlı	MAD.18131, p. 1

Gümrük-i İskele-i Bendereğli maᶜa Hasshâ-i Atik-i Bendereğli and *Zeâmet-i Reisülküttab (Chief of Scribes) Hamza Çelebi* mukātaᶜas, which were attached to the Royal domains before, were the mukātaᶜas were undertaken together (MAD.4689, p. 62). While Bendereğli mukātaᶜa consists of customs revenues, the other mukātaᶜas included Çak village of Yedidivan district and Kayadibi village of Amasrı district, which belonged to the hâs of Reisülküttab Hamza Çelebi. The iltizam price of the *Gümrük-i* İskele-i Bendereğli maᶜa Hasshâ-i Atik-i Bendereğli mukātaᶜa was 145,000 akçe on 30.08.1598. The iltizam price of the Zeâmet-i Reisülküttab Hamza Çelebi mukātaᶜa was 60,339 akçe on 28.02.1598. These two mukātaᶜas could not be offered to anyone for two years due to the incompetence of the former Nazir Bayram Çavuş. On 29.10.1600, four wealthy (agniyâ) people named Memi, Ali Hasan, Yusuf, and another Ali undertook these mukātaᶜas as iltizam (MAD.4689, p. 62). Çak village was later given to a man named Üveys Gürcü for 70,339 akçe for three years in 1603. Üveys Çelebi increased the income of the mukātaᶜa by 24,356 akçe during the three years. Moreover, there were no complaints from the people. This successful tax collector became the mukātaᶜa tax collector again in 1606 (MAD.5452, p. 148).

The last of the groups of mukātaᶜa to be offered together in Bolu were the three mukātaᶜas of Bolu, which were the revenues of *Mevkûfât*,[1] *Beytü'l-mâl-i Hâssa*[2], and *Hâsshâ-i Ifrâz-i Cedid*[3]. Previously, the revenues of Hâsshâ-i Ifrâz-i Cedid and Mevkûfât were tendered together to mültezims. Later, the revenues of Beytü'l-mâl-i Hâssa were included in this group. Mustafa Çavuş, who had been the nazir of Bolu in 1605, laid down as a condition that these revenues be collected by himself (MAD.5452, p. 3). It is most likely that the mukataᶜa of Beytü'l-mâl-i Hâssa was added to the other two mukātaᶜa after this date. In fact, the earliest records of this mukātaᶜa date from 1611 (MAD.4689, p. 28).

These three mukātaᶜas were tendered together by the nazirs and müfettişes. Although the iltizam price of each mukātaᶜa is written separately, the bid price is based on the sum of these three mukātaᶜa. When

[1] Mevkufât: vacant timars and later avariz taxes (Darling 1996, pp. 133, 316).

[2] Beytu'l-mâl-i Hâssa: revenue source coming from the estates of those dying without heirs and also estates of deceased members of the ruling class (Darling 1996, pp. 137, 196).

[3] The mukâtaᶜa consists of the revenues of 22 villages in various districts of Bolu. In 1569, Hâsshâ-i Cedid amounted to 100.500 akcas (Taş 1993, p. 64).

bidding, the bidder can choose to bid a certain amount for the three mukātaᶜa together, or a certain amount for each one. According to the first records in the defters, the revenues of first two mukātaᶜa were collected by emins in 1596 at a price of 430,000 akçe. However, as they had not been managed by an emin for a year and a half, the revenue from the treasury was not collected. In 1599, Musa, one of the whealty people (agniyâ) of Bolu, bidded 70,000 akçe more than the price of the mukātaᶜa and undertook for three years (MAD.4689, p. 56).

The tables below clearly show that after Musa, these mukātaᶜas were separately bidded. After Musa, Balı Çavuş bidded these mukātaᶜas in 1608 for 6 years with 100,000 akçe advance and 1,305,000 akçe in return. At the end of the fifth year, Balı Çavuş owed the state 3–400,000 akçe (MAD.1842, p. 18). Toward the end of the tahvil, Balı Çavuş bidded with 1,355,000 akçe by increasing 50,000 akçe for a new tahvil with Mustafa and 100,000 akçe advance for 6 years and won the tender (MAD.1842, p. 22). Meanwhile, Musa Çavuş undertook the mukātaᶜa as iltizam with 200,000 akça in advance and 1,375,000 akça in return (MAD.1842, p. 18; MAD.1850, p. 73). On 27 May 1614, Balı and Mustafa made a new offer, stating that they had won the tender before Musa Çavuş, but that Musa Çavuş had not paid the 100,000 akça in advance that they had paid in accordance with the contract. In this offer, they accepted Musa Çavuş's tender conditions as they were and won the tender. Later, however, Musa Çavuş made a new offer and succeeded in winning the tender (MAD.1847, p. 46; MAD.1850, p. 73). Considering the state's interest in the matter, it not only had an advance income of 200,000 akçe without taking any initiative, but also made a profit of 70,000 akçe in the mukātaᶜa price.

Musa Çavuş collected the revenues as a mültezim for about four years. During his time, he used to put pressure on people with his 70–80-man cavalry unit and collect taxes illegally. Müfettiş Şaban informed the Palace about the people's complaints with a written petition. Meanwhile, Mehmed bin Ibrahim, a resident of Göynük in Bursa, bidded to these mukātaᶜas. The Şaban stated that the people needed to be saved from the oppression of Mustafa Çavuş. Mehmed b. İbrahim's bid was 1,375,000 akçe for 6 years like Musa Çavuş. This bid was accepted on 26.06.1619 and Mehmed b. İbrahim became the new mültezim (MAD.7299, pp. 82–83).

These three mukātaᶜas were issued as one-year tahvils in 1624. There was no change in the iltizam prices of them. Hasshâ-i Ifrâz-i Cedid was bidded for one year at a price of 134,166 akçe, Mevkûfât at 55,833 akçe, and Beytü'l-mâl-ı hassa at 39,166 akçe. The emins of these mukātaᶜas respectively were Ali from the troops of Ebnâ-i Sipahiyan in 1624, Ali Hızır of the troops of the Silahdarân in 1626, and Kerim Mehmed from the troops of the Ebnâ-i Sipahiyan (MAD.3305, pp. 7, 28, 45). The following three tables provide detailed information on the three mukātaᶜa as I mentioned (Tables 4.7, 4.8 & 4.9):

The remaining mukātaᶜas of Bolu are typically managed independently. No information is available regarding the Gölvaroş mukātaᶜa. Conversely, the jizyas of the non-Muslims in Boyalı, which is a part of the Akçaşehir district that was annexed to the Havâss-ı Hümayun, the ihtisab and

Table 4.7 Mukātaᶜa-i Mevkûfât-i Livâ-i Bolu

Date (Hijri)	*Date*	*Period*	*Bid*	*Bidder (Mültezim)*	*Source*
01.01.1005	25.08.1596	3 years	100.000		MAD.4689, p. 28
01.01.1008	24.07.1599	3 years	120.000	Musa	MAD.4689, p. 56
01.01.1011	21.06.1602	3 year	120.000	Âmil-pây	MAD.4689, p. 63
01.01.1014	19.05.1605	3 years	125.000	Rıdvan Abdullah (Emin) Kurd Çavuş (kâbız-i mâl)	MAD.4689, p. 63; MAD.5452, p. 2,14
10.02.1016	06.06.1607	6 years	260.000	Kurd Çavuş	MAD.5452, p. 150
01.01.1020	16.03.1611	3 years	160.000	Balı Çavuş & Mustafa	MAD.1842, p. 22
01.01.1020	16.03.1611	6 years	330.000	Musa Çavuş	MAD.1842, p. 18
01.01.1023	11.02.1614	6 years	335.000	Musa Çavuş	MAD.1850, p. 73
01.01.1028	19.12.1618	6 years	335.000	Mehmed & İbrahim	MAD.7299, p. 82
01.01.1034	14.10.1624	1 year	55.833	Ali	MAD.3305, p. 7
01.01.1036	22.09.1626	1 year	55.833	Ali Hızır	MAD.3305, p. 28
01.01.1037	12.09.1627	1 year	55.833	Kerim Mehmed	MAD.3305, p. 45

Table 4.8 Mukātaᶜa-i Hâsshâ-i Ifrâz-i Cedîd

Date (Hijri)	*Date*	*Period*	*Bid*	*Bidder (Mültezim)*	*Source*
01.05.1005	21.12.1596	3 years	330.000		MAD.4689, p. 28
01.05.1008	19.11.1599	3 years	380.000	Musa	MAD.4689, p. 56
01.05.1020	12.07.1611	3 years	382.500	Balı Çavuş & Mustafa	MAD.1842, P. 22
01.05.1020	12.07.1611	6 years	805.000	Musa Çavuş	MAD.1842, p. 18
01.05.1023	09.06.1614	6 years	805.000	Musa Çavuş	MAD.1850, p. 73
01.05.1028	16.04.1619	6 years	805.000	Mehmed & İbrahim	MAD.7299, p. 82
01.05.1034	09.02.1625	1 year	134.166	Ali	MAD.3305, p. 7
01.05.1036	18.01.1627	1 year	134.166	Ali Hızır	MAD.3305, p. 28
01.05.1037	08.01.1628	1 year	134.166	Kerim Mehmed	MAD.3305, p. 45

Table 4.9 Mukātaᶜa-i Beytü'l-mâl-i Hâssa-i Liva-i Bolu

Date (Hijri)	*Date*	*Period*	*Bid*	*Bidder (Mültezim)*	*Source*
01.07.1020	09.09.1611	3 years	110.000	Balı Çavuş & Mustafa	MAD.1842, p. 22
01.07.1020	09.09.1611	6 years	235.000	Musa Çavuş	MAD.1842, p. 18
01.07.1023	07.08.1614	6 years	235.000	Musa Çavuş	MAD.1850, p. 73
01.07.1028	14.06.1619	6 years	235.000	Mehmed & İbrahim	MAD.7299, p. 82
01.07.1034	09.04.1625	1 year	39.166	Ali	MAD.3305, p. 7
01.07.1036	18.03.1627	1 year	39.166	Ali Hızır	MAD.3305, p. 28
01.07.1037	07.03.1628	1 year	39.166	Kerim Mehmed	MAD.3305, p. 45

ihzariye revenues of the Bolu district, and the dock customs of the Akçaşehir city center and its suburbs were consolidated and constituted a single mukātaʿa (MAD.4689, p. 57). The extracted information from the tax farm registers, written on the margin of the ihtisab contract, indicates that the income of Boyalu village was 6000 akçe. The total revenues of Bolu's ihtisab and ihzariye were also 6000 akçe, while Akçaşehir's dock revenues amounted to 5384 akçe, resulting in a combined total of 17,484 akçe. When a timar-holder Mustafa sought to undertake the mukātaʿa, it came to light that one of his colleagues had transferred his salary to the treasury and registered the mukātaʿa as a zeamet in his own. Subsequently, the zeamet was annulled, and Mustafa was granted a new zeamet for 200,000 akçe over a three-year tahvil. The nâzir's report is significant in determining the price of the mukātaʿa. According to the nâzir's report, the income of Boyalı was 60,000 akçe for a three-year tahvil, with an additional income of 80,000 from ihtisab and ihzariye for the same tahvil (MAD.4689, p. 57).

Two distinct mukātaʿa were established from the estate (hâs) of the Hacı Paşa. Hacı Paşa was a member of the Candaroğulları (Isfendiyarogullari) dynasty. Following the death of Hacı Paşa on 4 September 1587, the revenues allocated to him were annexed to the Hâvass-ı Hümayûn and collected by the emins (Katırancı 2022, pp. 90–94). The tahvil of Hacı Paşa Hass mukātaʿa, dated 27 February 1599, was being bidded for 260,000 akça. However, the bidding of the mukātaʿa was prevented by Müfettiş Bayram, and the revenues could not be collected. On 30 October 1600, the timar-holding Mustafa and Sefer undertook the iltizam, with 300,000 akça for a three-year tahvil (MAD.4689, pp. 28, 63).

The record dated 20/01/1597 of the mukātaʿa of Bedel village, located in the Eflani district of Bolu, indicates that the iltizam price is 16,500 akçe. This mukātaʿa is attached to the hâs of Hacı Paşa and bidded by an emin-mültezim Murtaza with 15,000 akçe (MAD.4689, p. 28). The mukātaʿa was managed collectively by Murtaza, his father and his brother. During this tahvil, Yusuf, a subject of him, undertook iltizam of the mukātaʿa by offering 16,000 akçe. Subsequently, on 21 August 1600, Mehmed, the resident timar-holder of the Eflani district, became the new mültezim of the mukātaʿa by bidding 20,000 akçe (MAD.4689, p. 61).

It is notable that during the period under examination, there were Jelali rebellions in Anatolia. One of the most significantly impacted regions by the rebellions was Bolu. To enhance the security of the city, the state employed a rather intriguing method. The castle at Taraklıborlu, now known as Safranbolu, was rebuilt. It had been captured by Sultan Orhan's son, Süleyman Paşa. Subsequently, the castle's strategic significance diminished following its incorporation into the city's fortifications under Ottoman rule, leading to its gradual deterioration. To mitigate the destructive impact of the Jelali rebels in Anatolia, a decision was taken to undertake repairs to this castle. 53 soldiers were deployed to the castle. The salaries offered to these soldiers was 80,000 akçe. To prevent the expenditure from being drawn from the state treasury, some revenues in Bolu were converted to a mukātaᶜa. And revenues of the mukātaᶜa was transferred to a fund for the salaries of these soldiers. This fund was constituted by a tax of 5 akçe levied on those engaged in the purchase and sale of saffron in the districts of Bolu, a share of the income generated by dye houses in the districts, a tax imposed on newly established water mills and the surplus income of Süleyman Paşa's vaqfs. The new mukātaᶜa was undertaken iltizam by Server bin Abdullah for a deposit of 50,000 akçe and a total cost of 242,136 akçe. Consequently, this new mukātaᶜa manifested as an identical revival of the castle (MAD.5452, p. 99).

The conditions set forth by tax farmers in tax farm contracts offer valuable insight into the dynamics of the relationship between the state and private entrepreneurs. This agent class, which farming taxes, assumed the role of an intermediary in the transfer of revenues to the central treasury. The data from the period and region under examination indicates that, although the majority of these entrepreneurs were from the military class, the wealthy were also interested in mukātaᶜas. It is therefore unsurprising that the identities of the bidders and the conditions they put forward in the contract are related to each other. From this perspective, an examination of the contract terms reveals that some expressions are essentially a written procedure, present in almost every contract. A tax farmer who operates two mukātaᶜas simultaneously can consolidate their accounting and utilize the surplus income of one to offset the deficit of the other[4]. Conversely, the tax farmer might seek to collaborate with individuals with whom he has a personal relationship[5]. Consequently, all officials, including havâle, katip, and the kâbiz-i mal, could appointed by the tax

4 "Mukâtaᶜât birbirinden ayrılmayub birinin fazlası birinin kesrine mahsûb ola."

5 "Küttâb ve hüddâm-ı sâ'ire dilediğimiz kimesneler ola."

farmer and he might pay salaries from the mukātaᶜa. If a nezâret is undertaking iltizam, the new nâzir is granted the prerogative of appointing any kâdî he deems fit as a müfettiş[6]. If these are timar-holders, it is also stipulated that their timars should not be taken away from them on the grounds that they did not participate in the wartime[7]. If an alternative bidder is successful in undertaking the mukātaᶜa of the recent tax farmer, the new tax farmer is obliged to pay the same advance sum as the previous tax farmer[8]. As these are general statements in a iltizam contracts, these do not include individual demands.

The conditions set out in tax-farming contracts provide insight into the expectations of private entrepreneurs vis-à-vis the state, beyond the mere right to collect income. In some cases, this may constitute a more senior-level assignment or a distinct income allocation. The limited number of examples that have been documented thus far provide insight into this phenomenon. One of the stipulations of the tax-farming contract pertaining to Nazir of Bolu Mukātaᶜas Bayram Çavuş was to be a sanjakbey of Ankara or Çankırı (MAD.4689, p. 28). Bayram Çavuş's request was deemed inappropriate. Mustafa, a resident of Bolu, who a tax-farmer candidate for the Mevkufat mukātaᶜa, sets conditions for himself and his personnel. He demands that he be permitted to retain his rank of çavuş, that one of his men be appointed to the position of troops member, and that the other be designated chief doorkeeper. Additionally, Mustafa asserts his intention to take five troops of soldiers with him to collect taxes, citing the presence of the Jelalis in Anatolia (MAD.5452, p. 2). The emin of the mukātaᶜa established for Taraklıborlu Castle, Sefer, has expressed a desire to assume the role of çavuş of Sultan's court (MAD.5452, p. 99). Collectively, these examples suggest that the emergence of a new agent class, in addition to acquiring the authority to collect state revenue, has also begun to shape an identity that makes individual demands of the state. As the state's authority in the provinces diminishes, the influence of the tax-farmer class is likely to grow, potentially leading to a shift in power dynamics.

[6] "istediğim kâdî tahvilim âharına dek müfettiş olub âhardân müfettiş olmaya."

[7] "sefer-i hümâyûna gelmedi deyu timârına dahl olunmaya."

[8] "Mukâtaᶜaya âhâr tâlib zuhûr idüp üzerimizden mukâtaᶜa kalkmak lâzim gelür ise virdüğümüz peşînimiz bize edâ eylemeyince mukâtaᶜa zabt itdirilmeye."

Consequently, studies on tax farm contracts during the period when the iltizam system was implemented provide the opportunity to contribute to both local history and Ottoman economic history of the Ottoman Empire. While the system as a whole is constrained by the limitations of contracts focused exclusively on a specific region, these studies provide invaluable insights into how the emergence of the tax-levy system is influencing the state and its constituent parts within society. Conversely, these contracts constitute a significant data source for regional studies. The increased utilization of the contracts, a significant source of economic data, in historical studies and regional histories will facilitate the acquisition of novel perspectives.

References

Primary Sources

MAD.d 4689; MAD.d 5452; MAD.d 1842; MAD.d 1850; MAD.d 7299; MAD.d 3305; MAD.d 18131; A.DVN.MHM.d 25, 28, 41, 42, 64; AE.SMMD.III 1/4; AE.SİBR 5/538.

Secondary Sources

Baer, G. (1986). Iltizam. In B. Lewis, V. L. Menage, C. Pellat & J. Schacht (Eds.), *The Encyclopaedia of Islam New Edition*, pp. 1154–1155. Brill.

Çakır, B. (2003). *Osmanlı Mukataa Sistemi (XVI–XVIII. Yüzyıl)*. Kitabevi Publishing.

Darling, L. T. (1996). *Revenue-Raising & Legitimacy Tax Collection and Finance Administration in the Ottoman Empire, 1560–1660*. Brill.

Faroqhi, S. (1994). Crisis and Change, 1590–1699. In H. İnalcık & D. Quataert (Eds.), *An Economic and Social History of the Ottoman Empire, 1600–1914 II*, pp. 411–636. Cambridge University Press.

Genç, M. (2022). *Osmanlı İmparatorluğu'nda Devlet ve Ekonomi 2*. Ötüken.

İnalcık, H. (1980). Military and Fiscal Transformation in the Ottoman Empire, 1600–1700. *Archivium Ottomanicum* 6, 283–337.

Katırancı, Ü. (2022). *Candaroğlu Ailesinin Osmanlı Sistemine Entegrasyonu: Bir Beylik Ailesi Secere Araştırması*. Ankara Hacı Bayram Veli University, Institute of Graduate Programs, Department of History.

Pamuk, Ş. (2021). *Osmanlı-Türkiye İktisadi Tarihi 1500–1914*. İletişim Publishing.

Tabakoğlu, A. (2020). *Osmanlı Mali Tarihi*. Dergah.
Taş, K. Z. (1993). *Tapu Tahrir Defterlerine Göre 16. Yüzyılda Bolu Sancağı*. Ankara University, Institute of Social Sciences, Department of History.

CHAPTER 5

Credible Commitment Obstacles to Early Modern State-Building: A Skeptical Overview

Ramiz Üzümçeker

Economists traditionally believed that long-run economic growth depended on democratic governance and secure property rights, but recent findings added state capacity to this list. Social scientists long argued that state capacity growth began in early modern Europe in response to the financial pressures of interstate conflict.[1] Later empirical research confirmed this causal link (Karaman and Pamuk 2013). Today, it is a consensus that those states that participated in frequent, violent, and burdensome wars truly came to raise more income per capita, but we do not know the precise mechanisms of this process. A famous explanation

R. Üzümçeker (✉)
Faculty of Social Sciences, Özyeğin University, Istanbul, Turkey
e-mail: ramiz.uzumceker@ozyegin.edu.tr

[1] The literature is extensive, but one of the earliest and most influential studies that made this argument was Tilly (1990).

B. Altay (ed.), *Revenue-Raising Institutions, State Organization and Economic Change in the Early Modern Ottoman Empire*, Palgrave Studies in Economic History,
https://doi.org/10.1007/978-3-031-96492-3_5

argues that the early modern monarchies suffered from a credible commitment problem: The monarchs failed to earn the lenders' trust that they would serve their debt, or the subjects avoided taxation since they did not trust that the government would spend the money in their interest. This reluctance on the taxpayers' side to finance government spending hindered fiscal capacity growth. The solution was to elevate their relative bargaining power so that they could force the monarch to abide by his promises in the future. In constitutional monarchies, parliaments with veto rights fulfilled this function, while in other places corporate bodies evolved to play a similar role. In countries where parties failed to develop such institutions, government revenues remained stagnant.

In this article, I revisit the main variants of the credible commitment argument. Focusing on the English case, I discuss the hypotheses that credible commitment mechanisms increased the government's borrowing capacity, that they fostered fiscal growth, and that credible commitment solutions benefited both central governments and tax-paying elites. The overall evidence offers a mixed picture, providing at best conditional support for credible commitment accounts. Next, I turn to credible commitment explanations of state capacity differences between absolutist monarchies. Such explanations strive to address why early modern absolutisms like France and Prussia increased central government income, whereas others like the Ottoman Empire and China fell behind. I examine the specific mechanisms proposed in the literature and ask whether they apply to the Ottoman institutions regulating revenue-farming and domestic borrowing. The Ottoman experience shows that reputation concerns and tacit insurance contracts could overcome credible commitment problems even if institutional remedies were absent. Furthermore, while the Ottoman political system contained no representative organs, elite alliances constrained the sultan's authority to a considerable extent. In this sense, the Ottoman sultans, if anything, were less free to break promises than French and Russian monarchs. This last observation constitutes a serious problem for any credible commitment account of fiscal capacity differences between absolutisms. I conclude that future modeling attempts must look for other mechanisms.

Credible Commitment Accounts

The scholarship on credible commitment is extensive, and studies typically treat multiple connected problems simultaneously. Below, I describe four distinct claims concerning the causal link between mechanisms of credible commitment and early modern public finances, and I address each in turn. First, did early modern monarchs' inability to credibly commit to contracts harm the governments' borrowing capacity? Second, did this problem block otherwise achievable permanent gains in fiscal income? Third, were institutional solutions to the credible commitment problem cooperative designs to extend governments' fiscal capacity? Fourth, does countries' differential success in solving the credible commitment problems account for all cases of fiscal capacity divergence? In other words, what does the model have to say about the divergences between absolutist monarchies?

War may have increased the monarchs' incentive to expand their fiscal bases, but it did not automatically imply a greater ability to do so. On the contrary, a monarch's instant need for cash sometimes pushed him to trade entitlement to future revenues for lump-sum receipts. Scholars argued that sales of offices and lifelong tax farming in Spain, France, and the Ottoman Empire all potentially eroded the governments' income sources in the long run (Thompson 1994; Ertman 1997; O'Brien 2011). In reality, these arrangements were not different from government borrowing in credit markets as long as the auctioning of farms and offices remained competitive (Bonney 1999; O'Brien and Hunt 1999). Of course, the governments expected to pay a default risk premium on interest in both loans and revenue entitlement transfers since their ex-ante commitment to serve their debt was not credible. For instance, the Spanish Crown repeatedly refused to fulfill its financial obligations in the sixteenth and seventeenth centuries and met a dramatically high market interest rate for it (Drelichman and Voth 2014). This propensity to default on accumulated debt by governments, the defenders of credible commitment accounts reasoned, was what prohibited substantial increases in early modern states' fiscal revenues. To make matters worse, creditors could not trust governments' promise to pay, as it was often more profitable for governments to renege on loans once the collection date arrived (Kydland and Prescott 1977). To increase their revenues, governments had to overcome this credible commitment problem.

Effects on Borrowing Capacity

North and Weingast (1989) saw post-1688 parliamentary voting on the public budget as key to solving the English crown's credible commitment problem. Accordingly, a parliamentary check on government action guaranteed that the crown would honor its debt in the future, which made lending to the English crown a reliable investment. North and Weingast's was a clearcut hypothesis that invited empirical testing, and researchers quickly set out to find out whether the Glorious Revolution was truly a watershed moment for English state finances. Many studies pointed out the institutional intricacies involved. Stasavage (2002, pp. 165–167) noted that credible commitment would function only if the Whig Party, representing creditors, held parliamentary control. He found evidence that sovereign credit risk indeed correlated inversely with the Whig majority. Cox (2011) argued that the critical institutional settlement in 1688 was ministerial responsibility, whereby a Whig majority could check the executive's overzealous spending tendencies by threatening with overthrow. Sussman and Yafeh (2006) demonstrated that the risk premium for English government debt remained high several decades after the Glorious Revolution, while O'Brien (1988) underlined the country's ability to raise more debt per capita than its rivals. Others questioned whether post-1688 governments really abstained from usurping property: Clark (1996) looked at the rate of return in private capital markets and found no statistically significant correlation between political climate and capital prices, the latter proxying the investment appetite. Hoppit (2011) argued that parliamentary legislation reinforced rather than prevented the violations of property rights; enclosures, compulsory transfer of public loss to private agents during the South Sea Bubble, the abolition of heritable jurisdictions, and the prohibition of slave ownership all constituted confiscatory practices. In a word, the government's commitment not to confiscate private wealth apparently did not turn out to be credible (Weingast 1993). The overall evidence is mixed, and the empirical support for the Glorious Revolution's positive impact on the Crown's credibility is mostly conditional on other factors. The parliamentary solution to the commitment problem may have boosted the government's borrowing capacity after all, but the newfound credibility still hinged on various political contingencies.

Effects on Government Income

Even if we grant that parliamentary control solved the government's problem of accessing credit, servicing a magnified debt load would still require permanent increases in public income. The empirical evidence on that front is also far from conclusive. O'Brien notes that the volume of the Exchequer's balance sheet continued to grow throughout the early modern era in England, but the decisive shift seems to have appeared earlier, during the Civil War and the Restoration (O'Brien 2011, pp. 425–428). On the other hand, Karaman and Pamuk (2013, p. 623) estimate in a counterfactual exercise that if England had had an absolutist regime instead of a constitutional one, its public revenues would have been visibly lower. This seems to lend indirect support to the credible commitment hypothesis, though with a caveat: The departure from the absolutist counterfactual only emerges from the 1750s onward. Overall, the authors posit that representative institutions became conducive to state capacity growth only in the more urbanized early modern societies where commercial classes impacted political outcomes. In contrast, absolutist coercion apparently performed better in the more predominantly rural societies (Karaman and Pamuk 2013, pp. 619–622). Dincecco (2008, 2011) also finds a positive correlation between parliamentary regimes and fiscal capacity, based on a nineteenth-century dataset. In brief, there is some evidence that the Constitution fostered fiscal capacity growth in England after 1688, but it is difficult to tell if it did so by solving the monarch's credible commitment problem.

The Question of Beneficiaries

The third issue is to decide whether credible commitment solutions were deliberate designs or unintended consequences. In this regard, one difficulty at the heart of the model is pinpointing what the consenting taxpayers gained from the arrangement. To be fair, a Whiggish parliament of creditors would no doubt be willing to push for fiscal reform since they wanted the treasury to repay their loans. But so would the typical financier of the old regimes in France, Spain, and Stuart England. A class of rentiers profiting from lending to the Crown existed everywhere; the problem is that their narrowly defined interests hardly overlapped with the broader strata of bankers, merchants, and other business owners. Whatever profit that the higher rentiers would expect, as long as the increase in the government's income exceeded per capita growth, the broader strata of bourgeois and middle classes were bound to bear a heavier fiscal burden. This is where the bargaining model of representation fails: Elites are trading political representation and thus veto rights over budgetary decisions in return for higher taxes, but representation is supposed to be a safety net against future threats to their benefits. What exactly are these benefits? (Boucoyannis 2015, pp. 306–307).

One answer might be a greater supply of public goods. Parliamentary checks might ensure that the executive spends the tax revenues on public welfare. The problem is that early modern polities hardly invested in welfare-enhancing public goods. Expenditures mostly consisted of war-making, debt service, and civic administrative spending to maintain the tax-collecting bureaucratic apparatus (Körner 1995; O'Brien 1988, p. 2). The question thus comes down to whether the army and the navy were public goods that benefited the English taxpayers. Pincus and Robinson answer this question affirmatively and argue that after 1688, the English Parliament fought the wars favored by the Whig Party. Accordingly, post-1688 English expansionism aimed at the uninterrupted colonial supply of industry raw materials and control of overseas trade routes. This sharply contrasted with the Stuarts' and continental powers' motives for war-making, which included glory and the spoils of territorial capture for the King and the nobles (Pincus and Robinson 2016). In brief, the urban industrial and commercial classes were willing to pay for public spending because they had ensured that government policy would serve their interests.

This reading of events is based on a particular interpretation of 1688 as the triumph of the English bourgeoisie planning to shape society according to the interests of commerce and industry (Pincus 2009, 2011). This is not the place to evaluate this hypothesis, defended most recently by Steve Pincus, from the lens of seventeenth-century English history; suffice it to say that historians of various persuasions unite in doubting whether 1688 really constituted a revolutionary break of the type described (Tapsell 2010; Pocock 2011; Coffman et al. 2013). Instead, the consensus is that the Glorious Revolution continued the agreement between the monied and landed interests reached in the Stuart Restoration.[2]

[2] For a classic Marxist account along these lines, see Hill (1961). For an example from economic history, see O'Brien (1988, pp. 425–426). Revisionism is a label traditionally

One might still argue that the constitutional check after 1688 precluded the formation of rent-seeking monopolies and office sales, thus placing state-building on a more efficient path in England (Ertman 1997). Pincus (2009, p. 388) makes a similar point concerning monopolies, although even he concedes that the East India Company is a noteworthy exception. However, the middle classes and business owners could never force the inner circle of notables to pay their share of taxes (O'Brien 1988, pp. 17–18). Excise taxes became the core item of government revenues, which meant that the bulk of the fiscal burden fell on domestic manufacturers, importers, and urban middle classes (O'Brien and Hunt 1999, pp. 72–73). Industrialists escaped their share of the burden only if they climbed to the higher echelons of the economic hierarchy, where the most powerful joined the landowners and financiers to make up an extended class of notables. The latter group continuously obstructed measures to introduce an income tax or reform the land tax until their surrender amidst the War of Second Coalition (O'Brien 1988, p. 18). This story is not dissimilar to the French and Habsburg Crowns' repeated failures to abolish the fiscal privileges of the upper classes in the eighteenth century (Capra 1995; Bonney 1999; Galabert 1999; Kwass 2000; Hochedlinger 2009). The Glorious Revolution does not seem to have made a great difference in this regard.

That is not to say that the post-1688 politics was a replica of the old regimes on the continent. There is conditional evidence pointing to some increase in English landowners' fiscal burden. O'Brien estimates that the direct taxes on agricultural income went up from 4–5% in 1670 to 20% in 1810, although Napoleonic Wars were responsible for much of this increase (O'Brien 1988, p. 15). Meanwhile, the pace of British economic growth definitely helped in easing the tensions over the distribution of fiscal burden: The disposable income of the middle classes continued to increase even after the more rapidly increasing tax payments were subtracted (Crafts 1985). Yet, these could only make the growing fiscal burden more bearable. It was only a select group of rentiers who claimed the material spoils of the constitutional agreement.

Scholars also question whether the monarch benefited from a constitutional solution to the credible commitment problem. It is true that a

applied to studies on early Stuart and Civil War eras, but their overall distaste for Whiggish accounts displays itself in their treatment of 1688 as well. For a summary of post-1970s trends, see Glassey (2013).

monarch might renege on his debt if he lost a war, but the creditors would add the risk premium to the interest. In effect, the parties would be agreeing on a debt-plus-insurance contract (Tomz 2007; Cox 2011). The model predicts that under the new system, the monarch would forego insurance, while the volume of credit would not change (Cox 2011, p. 137). The adherents of the credible commitment view can still argue that the constitutional check would be Pareto-improving because the monarch could avoid a high insurance cost. However, this might release some financial pressure on the income resources if the volume of credit remained constant, thus delaying rather than accelerating fiscal expansion. This would be the case if the monarch's demand for funds was inelastic—a realistic assumption provided that war pressure was largely exogenous. Alternatively, the monarch might choose to borrow less because of the higher interest rate. Overall, neither tax-paying elites nor monarchs are proven to have benefited from constitutional solutions to alleged credible commitment problems, even in theory.

Absolutist Monarchies

Other studies apply the credible commitment frame to absolutist regimes. Johnson and Koyama argue that the consolidation of revenue farmers into a corporate body in England (Great Farm) and in France (*Ferme generale*) was such a solution (Root 1989; Johnson and Koyama 2014). Accordingly, the collective action of revenue farmers threatened the monarch with multilateral punishment in case the latter reneged on promised payments to creditors, who also participated in corporate revenue-farming bodies. Since this solved the monarch's credible commitment problem, the total lending to the government grew (Johnson and Koyama 2014, p. 3). Johnson and Koyama's argument is sophisticated and supported by a rigorous model. However, they also rely on the absence of an insurance arrangement that would otherwise reestablish the borrowing market at some cost to the monarch. The authors compare an auction scenario where the monarch farmed out the revenues to the highest bidder to a Nash-bargaining frame where the monarch and a tax farmers' agglomerate shared the fiscal surplus. The former scenario involves a spot revenue-farming market with infinitely many bidders, who also happened to be the group of potential lenders to the crown. Crucially, the authors assume that the revenue-farming and credit markets were separate, so the monarch's default on debt would not hurt his reputation in the revenue-farming market. Yet this is arguably an artificial distinction since any revenue-farming contract was in effect a borrowing contract: a transfer of revenue entitlement was practically a promise to grant tax collection rights in the future. So why would the monarch honor this promise but not pay the debt? Would the credible commitment problem not apply to the revenue-farming market as well? Meanwhile, the monopsony power of the agglomerate would increase the tax farmers' profit at the monarch's expense. To the authors' credit, the consolidation of farmed-out revenue items was less a process of cartel formation than a state initiative in France, suggesting that the monarchs expected additional income from the arrangement (Johnson and Koyama 2014, pp. 8–9). On the other hand, the financiers in *Ferme Generale* did act as a political trust in forcing multiple reform-minded ministers to resign or concede during Louis XV's reign (Bonney 1999, pp. 154–156). In short, the negative distributional effect of farmers' agglomerates on government revenues is beyond doubt, whereas the positive allocational effect is, at best, arguable. This does not rule out the possibility that the monarch preferred greater borrowing capacity today to higher revenues in the long run, but it does require that he had a high future discount rate (Root 1989, pp. 252–253).

The Ottoman Case

Balla and Johnson (2009) apply a simpler version of the model described above to explain the divergence between French and Ottoman public revenues in the early modern era. Accordingly, Ottoman domestic borrowing fell behind France because they had no corporate body that integrated tax farms to solve the Sultan's credible commitment problem. Religious and ethnic heterogeneity of tax farmers in the Ottoman Empire probably made collective action difficult, though the decisive obstacle was the absence of the concept of legal personhood in Ottoman law (Balla and Johnson 2009, pp. 826–836).[3] The Sultan could not credibly commit not

[3] Balla and Johnson follow Timur Kuran's hypotheses to explain why similar corporations did not develop in the Ottoman Empire, see Kuran (2005a, 2005b). Of course, whether institutional inertia was truly an adequate cause for the observed absence of legal innovations is subject to debate, especially since the government would supposedly benefit from them. I leave the broader criticisms of Kuran's framework aside; for example, see Çizakça (2010).

to cancel revenue entitlements at will and resell the tax farms in the future, and the tax farmers refrained from entering long-term contracts.

As in the original model, Balla and Johnson (2009, pp. 6–7) assume that the debt-plus-insurance solution preached by Tomz and Cox was not applicable. However, a brief look at how the Ottoman *mâlikâne* system worked implies otherwise. The *mâlikâne* system, where multiple years' revenues were sold in advance through auction, was a combination of long-term domestic borrowing with revenue-farming (Genç 1975; Özvar 2003; Salzmann 2004). 42 Under this system, the winner of the auction paid a lump sum in advance (*muaccele*) and promised to pay a preset annual installment in three deliveries. In return, he would be entitled to the government's fiscal revenues from the income-producing unit (*mukataa*) in question in his lifetime. The *mâlikânes* gradually replaced earlier short-term tax-farming arrangements after 1695. The new system would hypothetically motivate the *mâlikâne*-holder to encourage productivity improvements since he could keep the additional revenue for himself. *Mâlikâne* shares circulated in capital markets, and the government started to charge a fifteen-percent *kasrıyed* fee on private sales in 1735 (Genç 2003). The system's downside was that the government gave up the expected income from future output growth in these *mukâtaas*. To be fair, the *mâlikânes* were not inheritable: They returned to the treasury as *mahlûlât* assets when the owner died. However, this only partly compensated for the government's incentive for future opportunism. The investors continued to confront the risk of contract violation by the government, which they probably considered when setting the auction price.

The Ottoman lump-sum receipts from *mâlikânes* must have reflected this discount for the buyer's future risk. The 1714–18 War with Venice and Austria pushed the Sublime Porte to temporarily cancel the *mâlikâne* contracts on sizable *mukâtaas* in the eastern provinces (Genç 1975). The government farmed out these *mukâtaas* again with around fifty-percent raises on their annual payment obligations. Genç interprets these increases as evidence that the *mâlikâne* system led to profit improvements. However, *mâlikâne*-holders would probably expect a discount in annual installments compared to ordinary tax farms in return for their lump-sum advances. Therefore, it is not entirely clear whether we can attribute the said increases to higher profitability. In 1717, the *mâlikânes* were offered to their former owners at half their earlier *muaccele* prices. Still, violating the investors' trust indispensably caused a dramatic decline in value in later sales. Indeed, Genç's calculations reveal an increase in the rate of return on *mâlikâne*-owners' investment from 25 to 35% in the 1730s, followed by a steady downward trend to about 15% by the early nineteenth century (Genç 1987, p. 350).[4] The author attributes this long-run decline to the government's persistent abstinence from breaking contracts, though it is difficult to know. Balla and Johnson point to premature terminations of short-term tax-farming contracts in the sixteenth and seventeenth centuries (see Çizakça 1993), but they do not compare them with the frequency of incidents in France. It is well-known that such confiscatory practices were common in France as well (Bonney 1999, p. 153).

This brief description of the *mâlikâne* system implies that the credible commitment problem did not inhibit the formation of a credit market where the government was the borrower. Rather, the government probably had to pay a risk premium on top of the equilibrium price. After all, bidders in *mâlikâne* auctions would not be willing to lower the charged interest rate below zero expected profit, and the expected profit would take the probability of default into account. The equilibrium volume of transactions may also have been lower than optimal if the degree of risk aversion varied in the population of bidders. In that case, those who were more risk-averse would refrain from *mâlikâne* contracts, and the government would fail to bring some capital into the *mâlikâne* system. This might explain part of the divergence between the Ottoman and French fiscal revenues. Of course, this would apply only to the individuals who were so risk-averse that the Pareto set of bilateral insurance contracts was empty, in which case the cost of credible commitment failure would be considerably lower. This is a general problem for the adherents of credible commitment accounts: In many cases, it is dubious whether the expected effect sizes are large enough to explain the observed differences in fiscal capacity.

A much more important problem was the tax farmers' inability to collect the promised revenue on the ground. One must remember that in the Ottoman Empire, the immediate purchasers of tax farms typically resided in Istanbul and subcontracted their entitlements to first their appointed servants and later local notables. Already in the sixteenth

[4] Studies on Ottoman credit markets demonstrated that government officers also confronted higher interest charges in their private transactions, possibly because lenders perceived the officers' ability to influence judicial processes as a risk factor (Kuran and Rubin 2018).

century, the treasury itself, the viziers, and the governors habitually farmed out their fiefs' (hâss) revenues to lower servants called *voyvoda* and *müteselllim* (İnalcık 1977, p. 30). In the seventeenth century, the share of imperial and vizier *hâss* increased at the expense of traditional fiefs (*timar*), which reinforced the provincial power of the *voyvoda* and *mütesellim* subcontractors (Barkan 1972; Cezar 1986; İnalcık 1997; Özvar 1998). In time, these servants either developed ties to the provinces or the local notables gradually replaced or sidelined them (Şimşek 2010, pp. 42–46). By the eighteenth century, local notables had almost monopolized the *voyvoda* and *mütesellim* posts. The process culminated in the rise of the *âyan* in the second half of the eighteenth century, but the *mâlikâne* holders' loss of revenues to the provincial agents probably started earlier.

It seems safe to say that the Ottoman state finances suffered more from a lack of incentive to overcome information asymmetries than a credible commitment problem. In selling *mâlikânes* to the highest bidders, the government typically transferred the right to collect taxes to private hands and thereby relieved itself of the incentive to impose fiscal centrism in the provinces. But the private *mâlikâne* holders were undoubtedly in a worse position than the government to intimidate the local fiscal intermediaries if they hoarded surplus (Şimşek 2010, pp. 37–38). In other words, a second-order credible commitment likely did not affect the tax-farming subcontracts. On the contrary, the balance of power gradually shifted in favor of the provincial actors.

However, perhaps the most problematic aspect of Balla and Johnson's model is their assumption that withholding future loans is the only way to punish a cheating monarch. In fact, the Ottoman *mâlikâne* owners as a group had various political apparatuses at their disposal to impose their will on the Sultan. To comprehend this point, note that *mâlikâne* purchasers almost exclusively came from the upper echelons of civil and military bureaucracy in Istanbul (Genç 1975; Özvar 2003). Today, it is a consensus among scholars that factions within the Ottoman bureaucratic elite became increasingly powerful from the late sixteenth century onward (Peirce 1993; Börekçi 2010). Conspiring groups in court and bureaucracy dethroned some six sultans between 1618 and 1730, and the higher officers blocked Osman II's and Mustafa II's attempts at absolutist rule (Abou-El-Haj 1984; Tezcan 2001). By the early 1700s, a network of pashas and other bureaucrats connected by household and family ties had mostly consolidated its rule (Tezcan 2010; Akbulut 2020, 2023). European travelers visiting the empire likened the constraints on the sultan's power to the English experience, while the political thinkers grasped this quasi-constitutional turn in real politics and reflected it in their writings (Yılmaz 2015). Although a formal constitution did not exist, the Ottoman Sultan was definitely less omnipotent than its French and Russian counterparts.

It would be unreasonable to assume that this political ability to check the monarch's decisions would not bring any bargaining power in *mâlikâne* contracts. One might object that usurping a few *mâlikâne* owners' revenue entitlements would not move the others toward cooperative punishment unless a corporate body to regulate collective action existed. However, in that case, the creditors would include the probability that the sultan would choose them for default in their risk calculation, and the cost of credible commitment failure would be considerably lower. Moreover, it would be arbitrary to require a well-defined economic punishment mechanism for the government's failure to abide by tax-farming contracts when other efforts to extract money from the elites' hands regularly met collective political resistance. The French experience is once again illustrative: French magnates' blockage of reform attempts by the likes of Turgot and Necker did not hinge upon *Ferme Generale*, nor was withholding credit their only available instrument. In any event, the Ottoman elite repeatedly proved capable of collective action against the sultan without a corporation or a representative body. Surely, they might design collective measures to prevent sultanic assaults on tax-farming contracts if they had the incentive.

This last objection to Balla and Johnson's model illustrates a broader problem with credible commitment accounts: They fail to explain the divergences in fiscal evolution between absolutist monarchies. In its original version, the credible commitment frame refers to constitutional checks over budget revenues as the explanatory variable and predicts that parliamentary control fosters fiscal expansion. Accounts like Balla and Johnson's constitute ad hoc qualifications to fit the model to observed irregularities. In doing so, they not only reduce the original model's appeal but also cause new incongruences with empirical knowledge, such as the claim that French monarchs in the Old Regime were more constrained by the elites than the Ottoman sultans. To point out the limits of Louis XIV's and Peter I's absolutisms is one thing, but one can hardly argue that Ahmed III or Mahmud I enjoyed greater freedom from elite interest groups in policy-making. At this point, to borrow the Lakatosian terminology, the credible commitment frame becomes a degenerating research program. Any account seeking to explain the difference between the Ottoman, French, and Russian fiscal capacities must look for answers elsewhere.

Conclusion

The origins of early modern state-building continue to attract economists' attention, and credible commitment accounts occupy an important place in their analytical toolkit. I argue that this privileged place is unwarranted. Credible commitment models have been fruitful in explaining fiscal capacity growth in constitutional monarchies, although closer scrutiny highlighted potential limitations and pitfalls even in this context. However, applications of the model to explain the capacity differences between absolutisms have so far been disappointing. This is because the central premise of the credible commitment accounts—the idea that early modern rulers' failure to raise income stemmed from an excess of unconstrained power—does not find support in the histories of low-capacity monarchies. This is also why further explorations along the credible commitment path do not promise meaningful progress. A better approach may be to search for other mechanisms linking war pressure to early modern fiscal growth.

References

Abou-El-Haj, R. A. (1984). *The 1703 Rebellion and the Structure of Ottoman Politics*. Nederlands Historisch-Archaeologisch Instituutte Istanbul.

Akbulut, M. Y. (2020). *XVIII. Yüzyıl Osmanlı Siyasi ve Sosyal Örgüsünde Bir Devlet Adamı Biyografisi: Hekimoğlu Ali Paşa (1689- 1758)*. PhD diss., 29 Mayıs University.

Akbulut, M. Y. (2023). Aileler ve Hâneler: Osmanlı Siyasi Yapısının Bir Tahlili (1703- 1766). In F. Öncel & S. Erdoğan (Eds.), *Osmanlı Tarihçiliğinde Yeni Çalışmalar: Kaynak,Bağlam,Yöntem*. Vakıfbank Kültür Yayınları.

Balla, E. and Johnson, N. D. (2009). Fiscal Crisis and Institutional Change in the Ottoman Empire and France. *The Journal of Economic History* 69 (3), 809–845.

Barkan, Ö. L. (1972). Tımar. *İslam Ansiklopedisi*, 286–317.

Bonney, R. J. (1999). France, 1494-1815. In R. Bonney (Ed.), *The Rise of the Fiscal State in Europe c. 1200-1815*. Oxford University Press.

Börekçi, G. (2010). *Factions and Favorites at the Courts of Sultan Ahmed I (r. 1603-17) and His Immediate Predecessors*. PhD diss., Ohio State University.

Boucoyannis, D. (2015). No Taxation of Elites, No Representation: State Capacity and the Origins of Representation. *Politics & Society* 43(3), 303–332.

Capra, C. (1995). The Finances of the Austrian Monarchy and the Italian States. In R. Bonney (Ed.), *Economic Systems and State Finance*. Oxford Universiry Press.

Cezar, Y. (1986). *Osmanlı Maliyesinde Bunalım ve Değişim Dönemi: XVIII. yy'dan Tanzimat'a Mali Tarih*. Alan.

Clark, G. (1996). The Political Foundations of Modern Economic Growth: England, 1540-1800. *The Journal of Interdisciplinary History* 26(4), 563–588.

Coffman, D., Leonard, A. and Neal, L. (2013). *Questioning Credible Commitment: Perspectives on the Rise of Financial Capitalism*. Cambridge University Press.

Cox, G. W. (2011). War, Moral Hazard, and Ministerial Responsibility: England After the Glorious Revolution. *The Journal of Economic History* 71(1), 133–161.

Crafts, N. F. R. (1985). *British Economic Growth during the Industrial Revolution*. Oxford University Press.

Çizakça, M. (1993). Tax-Farming and Financial Decentralization in the Ottoman Empire, 1520-1697. *The Journal of European Economic History* 22, 219–250.

Çizakça, M. (2010). Was Shari'ah Indeed The Culprit?. *MPRA Paper 22865 Uni- versity Library of Munich*, 1–48.

Dincecco, M. (2008). Fiscal Centralization, Limited Government, and Public Revenues in Europe, 1650–1913. *The Journal of Economic History* 69 (1), 48–103.

Dincecco, M. (2011). *Political Transformations and Public Finances: Europe, 1650–1913 (Political Economy of Institutions and Decisions)*. Cambridge University Press.

Drelichman, M. and Voth, H. (2014). *Lending to the Borrower from Hell: Debt, Taxes, and Default in the Age of Philip II*. Princeton University Press.

Ertman, T. (1997). *Birth of the Leviathan: Building States and Regimes in Medieval and Early Modern Europe*. Cambridge University Press.

Galabert, J. (1999). Castile, 1504–1808. In R. Bonney (Ed.), *The Rise of the Fiscal State in Europe c. 1200-1815*. Oxford University Press.

Genç, M. (1975). *Osmanlı Maliyesinde Malikane Sistemi*. Hacettepe Üniversitesi Yayınları.

Genç, M. (1987). A Study of the Feasibility of Using Eighteenth Century Ottoman Fiscal Records as an Indicator of Economic Activity. In H. İslamoğlu-İnan (Ed.), *The Ottoman Empire and the World-Economy*. Cambridge University Press.

Genç, M. (2003). Mâlikâne. *Diyanet İslam Ansiklopedisi*.

Glassey, L. K. J. (2013). In Search of the Mot Juste: Characterizations of the Revolution of 1688–9. In T. Harris & S. Taylor (Eds.), *The Final Crisis of the Stuart Monarchy: The Revolutions of 1688-91 in their British, Atlantic and European Contexts*. Boydell & Brewer.

Hill, C. (1961). *The Century of Revolution 1603–1714*. Thomas Nelson.

Hochedlinger, M. (2009). The Habsburg Monarchy: From 'Military- Fiscal State' to 'Militarization'. In C. Storrs (Ed.), *The Fiscal-Military State in Eighteenth-Century Europe: Essays in Honour of P.G.M. Dickson*. Routledge.

Hoppit, J. (2011). Compulsion, Compensation and Property Rights in Britain, 1688-1833. *Past and Present* 210(1), 93–128.

İnalcık, H. (1977). Centralization and Decentralization in Ottoman Administration. In T. Naff & R. Owen (Eds.), *Studies in Eighteenth Century Islamic History*. Southern Illinois University Press.

İnalcık, H. (1997). *An Economic and Social History of the Ottoman Empire 1300-1600*. Cambridge University Press.

Johnson, N. D. and Koyama, M. (2014). Tax Farming and the Origins of State Capacity in England and France. *Explorations in Economic History* 51 (1), 1–20.

Karaman, K. and Pamuk, Ş. (2013). Different Paths to the Modern State in Europe: The Interaction Between Warfare, Economic Structure, and Political Regime. *American Political Science Review* 107 (3), 603–626.

Körner, M. (1995). Expenditure. In R. Bonney (Ed.), *Economic Systems and State Finance*. Oxford University Press.

Kuran, T. (2005a). The Absence of the Corporation in Islamic Law: Origins and Persistence. *The American Journal of Comparative Law* 53 (4), 785–834.

Kuran, T. (2005b). The Logic of Financial Westernization in The Middle East. *Journal of Economic Behavior and Organization* 56 (4), 593–615.

Kuran, T. and Rubin, J. (2018). The Financial Power of the Powerless: Socio-economic Status and Interest Rates under Partial Rule of Law. *Economic Journal* 128 (609), 758–796.

Kwass, M. (2000). *Privilege and the Politics of Taxation in Eighteenth-Century France*. Cambridge University Press.

Kydland, F. E. and Prescott, E. C. (1977). Rules Rather than Discretion: The Inconsistency of Optimal Plans. *Journal of Political Economy* 85 (3), 473–491.

Peirce, L. (1993). *The Imperial Harem: Women and Sovereignty in the Ottoman Empire*. Oxford University Press.

North, D. and Weingast, B. (1989). Constitutions and Commitment: The Evolution of Institutions Governing Public Choice in Seventeenth-Century England. *The Journal of Economic History* 49 (4), 803–832.

O'Brien, P. (1988). The Political Economy of British Taxation, 1660- 1815. *The Economic History Review* 41 (1), 1–32.

O'Brien, P. (2011). The Nature and Historical Evolution of an Exceptional Fiscal State and its Possible Significance for the Precocious Commercialization and Industrialization of the British Economy from Cromwell to Nelson. *The Economic History Review* 64 (12), 408–446.

O'Brien, P. and Hunt, P. A. (1999). England, 1485-1815. In R. Bonney (Ed.), *The Rise of the Fiscal State in Europe c.1200–1815*. Oxford University Press.

Özvar, E. (1998). *XVII. Yüzyılda Osmanlı Taşra Maliyesinde Değişim: Rum Hazine Defterdarlığından Tokat Voyvodalığına Geçiş*. PhD diss., Marmara University.

Özvar, E. (2003). *Osmanlı Maliyesinde Malikane Uygulaması*. Kitabevi Yayınevi.

Pincus, S. (2009). *1688: The First Modern Revolution*. Yale University Press.

Pincus, S. (2011). The 1688 British Revolution: Political Economy and Radical Changes. *Revue D'histoire Moderne & Contemporaine* 58 (1), 7–52.

Pincus, S. and Robinson, J. (2016). Wars and State-Making Reconsidered: The Rise of the Developmental State. *Annales* 71 (1), 9–34.

Pocock, J. G. A. (2011). 1688: The First Modern Revolution (Review). *Common Knowledge* 17 (1), 186–189.

Root, H. (1989). Tying the King's Hands: Credible Commitments and Royal Fiscal Policy during the Old Regime. *Rationality and Society* 1 (2), 240–258.

Salzmann, A. (2004). *Tocqueville in the Ottoman Empire: Rival Paths to the Modern State*. Brill.

Şimşek, F. (2010). *Anadolu Sancaklarında Mütesellimlik Kurumu (XVIII. Yüzyıl)*. PhD diss., Akdeniz University.

Stasavage, D. (2002). Credible Commitment in Early Modern Europe: North and Weingast Revisited. *Journal of Law, Economics, and Organization* 18 (1), 155–186.

Sussman, N. and Yafeh, Y. (2006). Institutional Reforms, Financial Development and Sovereign Debt: Britain 1690-1790. *The Journal of Economic History* 66 (4), 906–935.

Tapsell, G. (2010). Not So Revolutionary. *The Review of Politics* 72 (4), 717–723.

Tezcan, B. (2001). *Searching for Osman: A Reassessment of the Deposition of Sultan Osman II (r. 1618-1622)*. PhD diss., Princeton University.

Tezcan, B. (2010). *The Second Ottoman Empire: Political and Social Transformation in the Early Modern World*. Cambridge University Press.

Thompson, I. A. A. (1994). Castile: Polity, Fiscality, and Fiscal Crisis. In P. T. Hoffman & K. Norberg (Eds.), *Fiscal Crises, Liberty, and Representative Government, 1450-1789*. Stanford University Press.

Tilly, C. (1990). *Coercion, Capital, and European States, AD 990–1990*. Basil Blackwell.

Tomz, M. (2007). *Reputation and International Cooperation: Sovereign Debt across Three Centuries*. Princeton University Press.

Weingast, B. R. (1993). Constitutions as Governance Structures: The Political Foundations of Secure Markets. *Journal of Institutional and Theoretical Economics (JITE) / Zeitschrift für die Gesamte Staatswis-Senschaft* 149 (1), 286–311.

Yılmaz, H. (2015). Containing Sultanic Authority: Constitutionalism in the Ottoman Empire Before Modernity. *Journal of Ottoman Studies* 45, 231–264.

CHAPTER 6

The Dawn of 5th Day in the Ottoman Empire: Nineteenth-Century Constitutional Regulations

Gencer Karabekir Karagenç

In one of the most desperate moments in the third film of Tolkien's immortal novel, The Lord of the Rings, adapted to the cinema by director Peter Jackson, the character Gandalf, one of the main characters of the series and played by Sir Ian Mckellen, tells his followers to look east at dawn on the 5th day of the war. Indeed, he played a very important role in winning the war by coming from the east with a large army at the dawn of the 5th day.

So, just like in the movie, what date corresponds to the dawn of the 5th day for the Ottoman Empire? What is the east to look at that day? This study aims to analyze the possibility of a victory based on the nineteenth-century Ottoman Constitutional developments. Because this victory, if

G. K. Karagenç (✉)
Faculty of Political Sciences, Ankara Yıldırım Beyazıt University, Ankara, Turkey
e-mail: gencerkarabekirkaragenc@aybu.edu.tr

B. Altay (ed.), *Revenue-Raising Institutions, State Organization and Economic Change in the Early Modern Ottoman Empire*, Palgrave Studies in Economic History,
https://doi.org/10.1007/978-3-031-96492-3_6

there is one, will serve as an important milestone in showing us the correlation between the Ottoman Empire and the state of law.

When we look at world political history from a general perspective, the first thing we encounter are sovereign states in which there is no separation of powers and no rules limiting the ruler. Afterward, police states emerged where the state set rules but did not comply with these rules. After police states, we encounter the treasury theory, in which the state and the state treasury are constructed as different legal entities. In its simplest form, in the treasury theory approach, the state does not comply with the rules it has set but compensates the losses resulting from its non-compliance from the treasury. After the treasury theory, the concept of the rule of law emerged. What is most generally meant by the concept of the rule of law is states that comply with the rules they set themselves.

In order for any structure to be considered a rule of law, it must meet various criteria. Elements such as judicial independence, financial responsibility of the administration, control of the constitutionality of laws, certainty and predictability of state activities, respect for acquired rights, and constitutional guarantee of fundamental rights and freedoms are among these criteria.

In this analysis, it was created in the Ottoman Empire in the nineteenth century; Constitutional documents such as *Charter of Alliance*, *Rescript of Gülhane*, and *Edict of Reform*, and regulations of the texts of the first constitution of the Ottoman Empire, were taken as basis. It was evaluated for what purpose the principles established through the mentioned regulations were made and to what extent the Ottoman Empire approached the concept of the rule of law in the modern sense.

General Political Situation of the Ottoman Empire in the Nineteenth Century

In many respects, the nineteenth century is called the century in which the process of collapse began for the Ottoman Empire. As stated in İlber Ortaylı's book about this period, which is a bestseller despite being written in an academic language, it is truly the "Longest Century of the Empire" (Ortaylı 2005, p. 2).

Ottoman political-administrative-military structure, XVI. It has entered a gradual deterioration process since the end of the century. In this disruption, wars defeats at the top played a dominant role. During this period, Continental Europe was experiencing the most radical transformations in its history. As a result of the change that occurred under the influence of the enlightenment philosophy, modernization, and industrialization resulted in necessary changes in the institutional structure of the Ottoman State.

Especially with the influence of the nationalist movement that spread after the French Revolution, many rebellions broke out, as in other multinational empires, and as a result of these rebellions, some communities gained their independence (Armaoğlu 1983, p. 6). In order to prevent the land losses resulting from this reason, the Ottoman Sultans who came to the throne after this date embarked on an intense reform movement.

Sultan Selim III, who ascended to the throne in 1789, undertook very important reforms, until 1808. During his reign, he made the first significant radical changes in the military and administrative fields. The innovations initiated by Selim I, especially in the military field, were continued by the subsequent sultans Selim III. The reforms targeted by Selim III were carried out by Sultan Mahmud II's reign, in a more institutional manner, including social, economic, and financial issues (Karal 2011, p. 80). It was transformed into a comprehensive innovation program. Published by Sultan Abdülmecit in 1839 with the imperial edict of Gülhane and Royal Edict of Reform, the Westernization movement became fully effective in the Ottoman geography.

As a general comment, the leadership of change in the Ottoman Empire was achieved by using state power. We can say that it was done by bureaucrats, intellectuals who wanted to modernize society, and students who studied abroad and then returned home. The main target policy in this change has always been the ideology of Westernization. In this context, they considered it necessary to integrate the institutions inherent in Western modernization into our system and built the revolutionary movements on this basis.

Charter of Alliance (Sened-i Ittifak)

In the Ottoman Empire, with the deterioration of the established political, administrative, and military order, the authority of the central government in the provinces was weakened of the state. The declining authority in the provinces was replaced by a local power that exceeded its authority. Officials and those who cooperate with them, called "landed proprietor (ayan) in Ottoman Empire" local forces were filling it (Ortaylı 2005, p. 42).

The "manoralizm (tımar) system" that trained Spahi soldiers (Zens 2011, p. 435). Due to corruption, the military support from the provinces to the central army decreased. In addition, cutting off the spoil revenues resulting from the defeats in the wars has increased pressure on the state (İnalcık 1995, p. 126). This resulted in the expenses not being covered. Systematic problems in the collection of taxes were another factor that worsened the economic situation.

Landed proprietor in Ottoman Empire under traditional Ottoman rule, they were a kind of provincial administrator, among the rich and influential people of the country. The main duty of the designated landed proprietor was to manage the relations between the public personnel carrying out military, administrative, financial, and economic public services, and the subjects. As the central authority of the state weakens, the landed proprietors, who became stronger, began to establish their own authority over the people. Especially since the first years of the nineteenth century, they were strong enough to negotiate with the central government. The powerful landed proprietors were, in a sense, even powerful enough to act independently of the central state authority. Establishment purposes aside, they turned into feudal lords.

After Sultan Mahmud II ascended the throne, landed proprietors were invited to Istanbul. The purpose of inviting the landed proprietors to Istanbul was to ensure that the local authorities, which had become stronger in the provinces and acted independently of the state, came under the authority of the central government again. However, during the negotiations, contrary decisions were taken (Jorga 2005, p. 200). The landed proprietors, who were not satisfied with the privileges they currently had, gained more autonomy and the privileges. They demanded new legal mechanisms to ensure their protection. Sultan reluctantly signed the Charter of Alliance on September 29, 1808, which restricted his absolute authority (Karal 2011, p. 93).

The signed contract generally contained the following provision (Gözübüyük and Kili 1985, p. 3-7):

- *Landed proprietors will show absolute loyalty to the Sultan's orders, and the Sultan will ensure the security of their property and life. If one of the landed proprietors opposes the Sultan, the other landed proprietors will side with the Sultan.*

- *Landed proprietors will help the state recruit soldiers. If there is an objection from the public against the recruitment of troops, the parties will jointly suppress those who oppose. against the enemies of the state, landed proprietors will fight together with the state forces.*
- *Collection of taxes to be collected from the states for the state treasury and the collected taxes are transferred to the center securely.*
- *The sovereignty of the state will be represented in the person of the Sultan. The orders of the Grand Vizier, who is the Sultan's deputy, will be obeyed just like the Sultan's orders. Grand Vizier in the laws and the signed deed if he goes beyond the promises made, the landed proprietors will resist.*
- *The existing rights of the in their regions will not end after their death but will be preserved by passing them on to their children. Landed proprietors cannot use force outside their own regions, cannot oppress the people, and cannot oppose the implementation of the law.*
- *If there are those in Istanbul or other military units who oppose the Sultan and cause chaos and rebellion, the land proprietors will come to Istanbul with their soldiers and help restore state authority.*
- *Citizens will be protected against all forms of cruelty and ill-treatment. The central government and landed proprietors will be able to act together to ensure public order and prevent ill-treatment.*

The Charter of Alliance is a text consisting of the 7 articles mentioned above and an annex. But it should be noted that none of its articles have been directly implemented. Sultan Mahmud II did not put any article into effect after fully establishing his central authority. Therefore, it can be easily said that the sole motivation for Sultan Mahmud II to sign this contract was to prevent a possible rebellion that might occur when he first came to the throne.

The Charter of Alliance has a very important symbolic meaning in Ottoman history, as it is the first constitutional document in Ottoman political history. In this respect, it is compared to Magna Carta in its doctrine (Akın 1980, p. 282). In addition, another importance of the Charter of Alliance is that it is the first document in Turkish political history that limits the powers of the ruler (Onar 1966, p. 147). However, despite these positive features, it should not be overlooked that this document is not a rule of law document. Because he gave the rights only to a certain group of landed proprietors, not to the whole people.

Rescript of Gülhane (Tanzimat Fermani)

Starting with Sultan Selim III and ending with the reform movements institutionalized with Mahmud II, every part of the country. Westernization efforts in the field continued. The aim of the reforms made in the military, administrative, and financial fields was to strengthen the central administration and make the authority of the state effective throughout the Ottoman geography. However, as in all projects inherent to humans, many unaccountable situations emerged here as well in political movements imposed from the top rather than from the bottom. The gateway to the Western world, not only bureaucratic reform movements came to the country. Moreover, revolutionary ideas such as freedom, equality and freedom, which are the leading engine of change in Europe (Grimm 2016, p. 4). It found a serious base, especially among the educated young generations of the state.

The process of following Western ideas, which started in the translation rooms in order to learn Western languages, gained momentum with the return of students sent to Western schools for education. Especially the high-level bureaucrats of the state were now appointed among the names that went through these processes. This ensured that ideas belonging to Western ideology dominated the state's decision-making processes.

In such a political environment, the Rescript of Gülhane was declared by Sultan Abdülmecid, who was also a supporter of innovation and ascended to the throne after Mahmud II. The edict was first read and announced to the public and foreign representatives in Gülhane Park on Novermber 3, 1839 by the Grand Vizier of the period, Mustafa Reşit Pasha, who also served as an ambassador in Paris and London. That's why the name of the edict is Rescript of Gülhane (Davison 2021, p. 47).

The regulations in the Rescript of Gülhane can be summarized as follows (Karatepe 2018, p. 12):

- *Security of life, chastity and honor will be provided to all Ottoman subjects, regardless of religion or nationality.*
- *Everyone will have the right to own property. No one's property will be confiscated through illegal means.*
- *Fair rates for taxes will be assigned. Equality will be ensured among citizens in the distribution of the tax burden.*
- *Military service will be limited to a certain period of time. A number of soldiers will be recruited in proportion to their population.*

- *The property of criminals will not be confiscated, and their heirs will not be deprived of inheritance.*
- *Civil servants will be paid salaries from the treasury. Bribery will be prohibited and those who do not comply with this prohibition will be punished.*

As can be seen from the articles, with the Rescript of Gülhane principles such as the principle of protecting the life, property, and chastity of the people, the legality of crimes and punishments, the publicity of the trial, the prohibition of general confiscation, the principle of equality, and the right to property entered the Ottoman legal system (Berkes 2012, p. 222). However, this should not be interpreted as if these principles were not implemented in the Ottoman Empire before. These principles, which were stated only with the Rescript of Gülhane, were legally guaranteed under a constitutional document (Aldıkaçtı 1978, p. 46).

The Rescript of Gülhane is considered the first step in the transition to a rule of law for the Ottoman Empire (Tanör 2009, p. 214). The reason why the Rescript of Gülhane not the Charter of Alliance is accepted as the document of the state of law is that it gave the rights it brought to all subjects. As stated, the Charter of Alliance granted rights only to a certain group of landed of proprietors (Onar 1966, p. 149).

Edict of Reform (Islahat Fermani)

As mentioned before, one of the main purposes of all the reforms made in the nineteenth century was to prevent the rebellions that emerged as a result of the nationalist movements brought about by the French Revolution. Because Western states were trying to intervene in the internal affairs of the state by provoking the minorities within the Ottoman Empire (Akyıldız 2011, p. 3).

Sultan Abdülmecid, who could not get the results he wanted with the reforms carried out with the Rescript of Gülhane decided to issue a second edict, especially regarding minority rights. For this purpose, the Edict of Reform was published in 1856. The edict generally included the following points (Tanilli 1962, p. 15):

- *The legal equality of all citizens, Muslim and non-Muslim, will be accepted.*

- *The elected patriarch will serve for life and will be the new member of the patriarchate. Assemblie can be established.*
- *New schools and places of worship can be opened in cities and towns where non-Muslim communities live.*
- *Citizens in entering the public service and being drafted into the military equality will be observed between them.*
- *The state will be treated fairly when collecting taxes. By way of farming contracts tax collection will be stopped.*
- *Jizya tax will be abolished.*
- *European capital will be used in development. Foreigners could own property in the Ottoman country.*

As can be seen, with the Reform Edict, non-Muslims were given the opportunity to become civil servants and soldiers, and the jizya tax, which was collected from non-Muslims in return for not enlisting in the military, was also abolished.

In particular, the ability of non-Muslims to take part in the military/civil bureaucracy was a revolutionary development for the Ottoman Empire. The Ottomans had previously assigned young and intelligent non-Muslim children to work in the bureaucracy in the places they conquered. However, before they reach important bureaucratic positions, they first convert these children to Muslims through the method we call devsirmeh and subject them to a strict training process. However, it should be noted at this point that providing non-Muslims with the opportunity to become soldiers is not a situation that is desired or desired by non-Muslim subjects. The fact that non-Muslim subjects did not have the opportunity to work in the bureaucracy for many years led them to specialize in professions such as tradesmen and craftsmen and enabled them to retain the limited capital accumulation in the Ottoman Empire. However, as being able to take part in the military bureaucracy is a regulation that also includes compulsory military service, it was not welcomed in the non-Muslim community (Lewis 2008, p. 127).

The importance of the Edict of Reform in Turkish political history is that it provided legal equality for the first time. In the Ottoman Empire, the legal equality of Muslims and non-Muslims was secured for the first time through a constitutional document.

Declaration of the First Constitutional Monarchy (Kanun-i Esasi)

The Tanzimat reforms carried out in the nineteenth century did not produce the desired results. Neither the relations with Western states nor the expectations of the non-Muslim subjects were met at the desired level (Şentop 2005, p. 652). For this reason, the intervention of Western states in the internal affairs of the Ottoman Empire continued (Tunaya 2015, p. 242). However, it would not be fair to say that these reforms did not contribute at all. These reforms paved the way for the formation of an institutional opposition through a new intellectual class in the country.

This formation, called the Young Ottomans, carried out an effective opposition by focusing on the rights brought by the constitutional developments in the West. The New Ottomans had a goal of a constitutional monarchy similar to that in the West. In this context, they wanted a system in which the sultan's powers were limited and the parliament was effective. In this context, their opposition quickly evolved into a constitutional regime movement.

The first constitution of the Ottoman Empire was prepared under these conditions under the leadership of Mithat Pasha and put into effect with the approval of the Sultan on December 23, 1876 (Onar 1966, p. 150). This date also meant the declaration of the first Constitutional Monarchy for the Ottoman Empire. The Ottoman Empire was now governed by a constitutional monarchy government system on paper.

The 1876 Constitution was prepared by taking the Belgian, Prussian, and Polish constitutions as examples rather than the French Constitution. The general features of the Constitution can be listed as follows (Yılmaz 2007, p. 259):

- *It consists of 119 articles.*
- *It was established in a strict and casuistic format.*
- *It is stated in the constitution that the capital is Istanbul, the state religion is Islam, and the official language is Turkish.*
- *Many fundamental rights and freedoms regarding personal and political rights are included in the constitution.*
- *Regulations regarding the judicial organization are included in the constitution.*
- *It is stated that the state structure is unitary.*

The 1876 Constitution adopted a constitutional monarchy as a government system and envisaged a dual parliamentary structure. These assemblies were called the assembly of citizen (Meclis-i Mebusan) and assembly of landed proprietors (Meclis-i Ayan). While the members of the assembly of citizen were elected by the people, the members of the assembly of landed proprietors were determined by the Sultan.

The first version of the 1876 Constitution gave the sultan very broad powers that could not be reconciled with the separation of Powers. The sultan had a wide range of powers, from exiling opponents to dissolving the parliament. He also had absolute veto power over laws. Members of parliament were required to obtain permission from the sultan before proposing a bill (Abadan and Savcı 1959, p. 38).

We must say that the first version of the 1876 Constitution was not a constitutional monarchy in the Western sense, considering the broad powers it gave to the sultan. Because in the classification of government systems, in a constitutional monarchy, which is classified as a type of monarchy under the union of powers, it is essential for an authorized assembly to be present next to the sultan. However, both the powers granted constitutionally and the principle of limiting the powers of the sultan, as seen in practice, could not be put into practice. Therefore, although the constitutional monarchy system was regulated in words, it remained on paper.

One year after the opening of the parliament, Abdulhamid II sent the parliament into indefinite recess, citing the war between the Ottoman Empire and Russia as the reason (Aldıkaçtı 1978, p. 62). This recess lasted until the declaration of the Second Constitutional Monarchy in 1908. In Ottoman political history, this 32-year period is called the period of autocracy.

Abdulhamid II is one of the most controversial sultans in Ottoman political history. During his long reign, some called him the Red Sultan and others the Great Khan. His long reign has taken its place in history as a period when Westernization projects continued but libertarian movements were also suppressed.

With the twentieth century, another structure became effective in the Ottoman state administration. This group, called the Committee of Union and Progress (İttihat ve Terakki), took over the administration completely and ensured the declaration of the Second Constitutional Monarchy in 1908. After the declaration of the Second Constitutional Monarchy, amendments were made to the 1876 Constitution in 1909.

The main changes made to the Constitution in 1909 can be listed as follows (Gözübüyük and Kili 1985, p. 109):

- *The sultan's absolute veto and dissolution power of the parliament were limited.*
- *The requirement to obtain permission from the Sultan for a bill has been abolished.*
- *Censorship in the press is prohibited.*

The importance of these changes in terms of Ottoman political history is that the Ottoman Empire became a constitutional monarchy in the Western sense. The reason why the Western constitutional monarchy began with the 1909 constitutional amendments, not with the first version of the 1876 Constitution, was that a truly competent parliament now existed both in theory and in practice (Eroğul 2016, p. 189). The existence of a ruler with relatively limited powers also made decisions more democratic when the conditions of the period were taken into consideration (Arsel 1959, p. 330).

Conclusion

The nineteenth century was a century full of political turmoil for the Ottoman Empire. This situation was caused by both developments in foreign policy and instabilities in domestic politics. This period was a period in which the path to the collapse of the state accelerated under the influence of global developments.

The nationalist movement that spread especially after the French Revolution deeply affected multinational empires such as the Ottoman Empire, and rebellions broke out in many parts of the Ottoman geography. In fact, the underlying reason for all the democratic efforts of the Ottoman Empire was the effort to prevent rebellions and prevent the disintegration of the state.

The Charter of Alliance was the regulation that was created in the nineteenth-century Ottoman constitutional regulations without a macro purpose, just to save the day. It appears as a forced regulation that the newly ascended Sultan Mahmud II had to sign until he could establish his own central authority. It has symbolic importance only because it is a regulation that limited the authority of the ruler for the first time in

Ottoman political history, and in this respect, it resembles Magna Carta. However, as stated, it should not be accepted as a document of the rule of law, as it only grants rights to the landed proprietors.

Rescript of Gülhane, the second constitutional document in the nineteenth century, is a milestone in the history of the Ottoman Empire as it secured many fundamental rights and freedoms under a constitutional text, from property rights to various principles of prosecution, from provisions on crimes and punishments to public security. Since these rights were granted to all subjects, the Rescript of Gülhane is considered the first step toward a state governed by the rule of law.

The third constitutional document of this century, the Reform Edict, is a regulation that was created specifically for minority rights. By abolishing the jizya tax and providing non-Muslims with the opportunity to become civil servants and soldiers, it provided legal equality between Muslims and non-Muslims for the first time in Ottoman political history.

These two decrees, published during the reign of Sultan Abdülmecid, aimed to prevent possible rebellions by minorities rather than to institutionalize freedoms in the Ottoman Empire. Although the rights-based demands of bureaucrats and intellectuals influenced by freedom movements in the West undoubtedly played a role in the publication of the decrees, the main purpose was always to prevent foreign states from interfering in the internal affairs of the Ottoman Empire.

The first constitution of the Ottoman Empire, the 1876 Constitution, was established under the pressure of an institutional opposition, unlike other regulations. The first constitution was prepared under the influence of the Young Ottomans, which we can call an organization of young people and intellectuals sent to Europe for education. The aim of following constitutional developments in the Western world conjuncture is also an important source of motivation. The constitution, while containing many regulations regarding personal and political rights, was designed in a rigid and casuistic format. Although the first version of the 1876 Constitution aimed for a constitutional monarchy as a government system, it could not achieve this due to the powers given to the sultan, such as absolute veto, dissolution, exile, and the fact that bills of law were subject to the sultan's permission.

Following the parliament being sent on an indefinite recess citing the Ottoman-Russian War and the 32-year autocracy of Sultan Abdulhamid II, the 2nd Constitutional Monarchy was declared in 1908, and the 1909 amendments were made to the 1876 Constitution. With these amendments, the sultan's exile authority was abolished, and his veto and termination powers were limited. With these amendments, the parliament became truly authorized, and the sultan's powers were also limited. Thus, the Ottoman Empire transitioned to a constitutional monarchy in the Western sense.

In sum, the constitutional developments, and regulations in the Ottoman Empire in the nineteenth century were primarily aimed at preventing the collapse of the state. In order to prevent rebellions and to re-establish public security, reforms were carried out, especially by targeting minorities. In this way, it was aimed to prevent Western states from interfering in our internal affairs. The internal demands regarding constitutional reform were limited to the Westernization motivations of a limited bureaucratic group, intellectuals, and students sent to the West.

References

Abadan, Y. and Savcı, B. (1959). *Türkiye'de Anayasa Gelişmelerine Bir Bakış*. Ankara Üniversitesi Siyasal Bilgiler Fakültesi Yayınevi.

Akın, İ. *Kamu Hukuku*. İstanbul Üniversitesi Hukuk Fakültesi Yayınları.

Akyıldız, A. (2011). Tanzimat. *İslam Ansiklopedisi* 40, 1–10.

Aldıkaçtı, O. (1978). *Anayasa Hukukumuzun Gelişmesi ve 1961 Anayasası*. Fakülteler Matbaası.

Armaoğlu, F. (1983). *20. Yüzyıl Siyasi Tarihi (1914–1980)*. Türkiye İş Bankası Yayınları.

Arsel, İ. (1959). *Türk Anayasa Hukuku*. Mars Yayınevi.

Berkes, N. (2012). *Türkiye'de Çağdaşlaşma*. Yapı Kredi Yayınları.

Davison, R. (2021). *Osmanlı İmparatorluğunda Reform 1856–1876*. Dergâh Yayınları.

Eroğul, C. (2016). *Anatüzeye Giriş*. İmaj Yayınevi.

Gözübüyük, Ş. and Kili, S. (1985). *Türk Anayasa Metinleri*. Türkiye İş Bankası Yayınları.

Grimm, D. (2016). *Constitutionalism: Past, Present, and Future*. Oxford University Press.

İnalcık, H. (1995). *Political Modernization in Turkey, in From Empire to Republic*. ISIS Press.

Jorga, N. (2005). *History of the Ottoman Empire*. Yeditepe.

Karal, E. Z. (2011). *Osmanlı Tarihi V*. TTK Yayınları.

Karatepe, Ş. (2018). *Türk Anayasa Hukuku*. Savaş Yayınları.

Lewis, B. (2008). *The Emergence Of Modern Turkey*. Arkadaş.

Onar, S. S. (1966). *İdare Hukukunun Umumi Esasları*. Hak Kitapevi.

Ortaylı, İ. (2005). *İmparatorluğun En Uzun Yüzyılı*. İletişim.

Şentop, M. (2005). Tanzimat Dönemi Kanunlaştırma Faaliyetleri Literatürü. *Türkiye Araştırmaları Literatür Dergisi* 5, 647–672.
Tanilli, S. (1962). *Anayasalar ve Siyasal Belgeler*. Cem Yayınevi.
Tanör, B. (2009). *Osmanlı-Türk Anayasal Gelişmeleri*. Yapı Kredi Yayınları.
Tunaya, T. Z. (2015). *Türkiye'de Siyasal Partiler*. İletişim.
Yılmaz, F. (2007). Türk Anayasa Tarihi. İz Yayıncılık.
Zens, R. (2011). Provincial Powers: The Rise of Ottoman Local Notables (Ayan). *History Studies* 3(3), 433–447.

PART II

Theorizing Taxation in the Ottoman Past

CHAPTER 7

Introduction: A Theoretical Background

Metin M. Coşgel

Throughout history, states used tax farming as a system of tax collection in which private agents were granted the right to collect taxes on behalf of the government. Instead of the state directly collecting taxes, it would auction or assign the right to collect taxes to a third party, who would pay the government a fixed sum up-front and then recoup their investment (and ideally a profit) by collecting taxes from the population or the producer. The earliest known examples of tax farming date back to Ancient Egypt and Mesopotamia, where officials were granted the right to collect taxes on trade, manufacturing, and agricultural production. In Ancient Greece, the system was similarly used in city-states such as Athens, where tax collectors, known as *telonai*, bid for the right to collect customs duties and other taxes. Republican Rome began to give out tax-farming contracts (*publicani*) through auctions as early as the third century B.C. (Levi 1988, Ch. 4). This type of contract was also used by Medieval states such as the Abbasid Empire, a precedent followed by other Islamic

M. M. Coşgel (✉)
The University of Connecticut, Storrs, USA
e-mail: metin.cosgel@uconn.edu

B. Altay (ed.), *Revenue-Raising Institutions, State Organization and Economic Change in the Early Modern Ottoman Empire*, Palgrave Studies in Economic History,
https://doi.org/10.1007/978-3-031-96492-3_7

states under the *iqta* system (Løkkegaard 1950, Ch. 4). Tax farming was common in medieval and early modern Europe, particularly in France, Spain, and the Holy Roman Empire. More recently, rent contracts have been observed in modern day Tunisia for the collection of taxes from periodic (mostly weekly) markets (Azabou and Nugent 1988, 1989). Though tax farming is largely obsolete today, some modern practices bear similarities, such as private companies collecting tolls, fees, or even managing outsourced government tax collection efforts.

The Ottoman Empire was no exception to the contemporary historical trend of relying heavily on tax farming for the collection of certain revenues (Akdağ 1959, pp. 231–247; Çizakça 1996, Ch. 5; Darling 1996, Ch. 4; Salzmann 1993). Under a system called *iltizam*, the state sold the right to collect taxes to private agents (called *mültezims*). From the fifteenth to the nineteenth centuries, it was a key fiscal institution in an empire that spanned vast and diverse territories and extracted revenues from several types of sources. Along with other methods of text-collection, it was part of a sophisticated system that allowed the state to collect revenues efficiently, as detailed in other chapters of this volume.

The objective of this chapter is to provide a theoretical background to tax farming. I first offer a simple economic model of tax collection that differentiates among methods of tax collection in terms of the cost and benefits of implementing them. I then use this comparative framework to determine the conditions under which a government would choose tax farming over other methods of tax collection. Finally, I use the model to discuss the changing feasibility of tax farming over time and reasons for switching to alternative methods.

A Simple Model of Tax Collection

Suppose the amount of tax revenue that can be collected over a set period of time is determined by the production function

$$R = f(e)B \tag{7.1}$$

where e is the effort of a risk-neutral tax collector and B is the tax base. We assume that B is unobservable both to the government and the collector, and e is unobservable to the government. The government (or would be collectors) can, however, learn the values of B, R, and e by investing in the appropriate measurement technology. Specifically, it can measure the tax base by incurring a fixed cost *m* before the tax is collected; it can measure the actual tax by incurring a fixed cost *k* after the tax is collected; and it can observe the collector's effort by spending *s(e)* on monitoring.[1]

The government faces a standard principal-agent problem in that it must design an incentive scheme to elicit effort from the collector. The specific characteristics of the scheme will depend on which variables the government decides to measure, as this determines the information on which the parties can contract and the consequent cost of implementation. We can categorize historically observed schemes of tax collection into three groups depending on whether the government measures the tax base (*B*), the actual tax collected (*R*), or the collector's effort (*e*). In contractual terms, these schemes are called tax farming, share contract, and wage contract.

For a specific source of revenue, the government's choice of a collection scheme will depend on its expected net revenue. Under a tax-farming contract, the government measures *B* up-front at cost *m* and allows the agent to collect taxes based on the promise to pay the government a pre-specified amount. Since the tax farmer receives the residual, this arrangement has the inherent advantage that effort is efficient for all realizations of *R*. Consider next the share contract, in which the government measures the actual tax collected, *R*, and then shares that amount (and the consequent risk) with the collector according to a pre-arranged sharing rule. To ensure that it fully receives its share, the government must incur *k*. Finally, under a wage contract, the government incurs *s* to measure the collector's effort and receives *R* minus the wage payment.

Figure 7.1 shows the three schemes of tax collection as functions of *k* and *s*. To understand when a government would choose tax farming, we can compare the three schemes in terms of which yields the highest expected return to the government. Consider first the comparison between the share contract versus the wage contract. In neither case is effort state contingent, so the comparison depends only on the relevant measurement costs. The nature of the costs differs, however: under the share contract it is fixed and hence non-distortionary, whereas under the wage contract it is proportional to effort and therefore distortionary. In both cases, however, as the measurement cost goes to zero, the expected

[1] For the assumptions, derivation, and full details of this model, see Coşgel and Miceli (2005), on which this chapter is based. See also Coşgel (2005) for the Ottoman tax system and examples of personal, production, and trade taxes.

return converges to the efficient level. Thus, for sufficiently high *k* the wage contract dominates, while for sufficiently high *s*, the share contract dominates. This is illustrated in Fig. 7.1, where the positively sloped locus in (*k*,*s*) space demarcates the relevant regions for the two contracts. Specifically, the wage contract dominates for points above the line (high *k*), and the share contract dominates for points below the line (high *s*).

Now introduce the tax-farming contract. As noted above, this arrangement has the inherent advantage that effort is both state contingent and efficient. Thus, if the up-front cost of measuring the tax base, *m*, is sufficiently low, the rent contract will dominate both of the other arrangements. This is indicated in Fig. 7.1 by the vertical and horizontal lines, which show that the rent contract dominates for large enough values of *s* and *k*.

The figure also shows what happens when the variance or cost of measuring *B* changes. The solid lines demarcate the relevant regions for a given value of *m* and holding the variance of *B* fixed. However, an increase in the variance of *B* will increase the value of state-specific effort. The dashed lines show what happens in this case. Since only the rent contract induces state-contingent effort, an increase in the variance of the tax base will expand the region where it dominates relative to wage and share contracts. In contrast, the region where the rent contract dominates will contract as the cost of measuring *B* increases.

Fig. 7.1 Choice of tax collection schemes

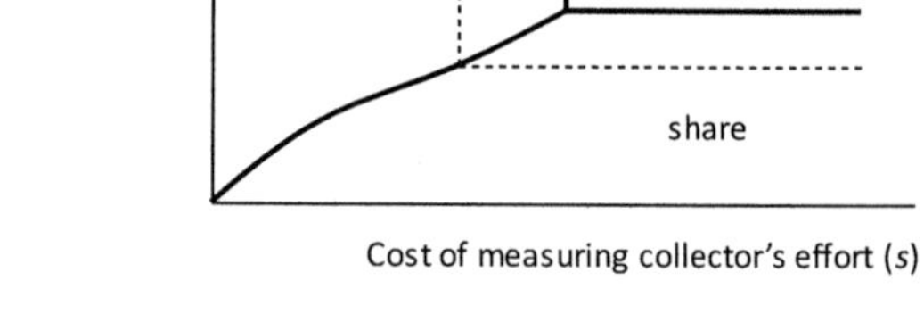

Why Tax Farming?

To see how the model helps to explain historical reality, consider first a hypothetical case of an invariant tax base (i.e., the variance of B is zero), where the government can also measure the tax base and tax revenue at no cost ($m = k = 0$) and can observe the collector's effort perfectly ($s = 0$). This is similar to the case of poll taxes (a fixed amount per person) from an unchanging small population known with certainty. In that case, the Coase theorem would imply that it would not matter which contractual form the government would choose to collect taxes. Any of the three available methods could be used, with identical outcomes for e and R.

In reality the tax base would typically be variable for most taxes, and the cost of measuring the collector's effort, the tax base, and tax revenue would be positive. In that case, the model would predict the government to choose tax farming over wage or share contracts if the cost of measuring the tax base was low and the variance of the tax base and the cost of measuring effort and tax revenue were high.

A common explanation of tax-farming contracts offered in the literature has been that they were preferred over wage contracts when the cost of measuring the collector's effort was too high. This type of explanation has been commonly given for the observed incidence of tax-farming contracts in France, England, and Tunisia, among other places. Another common explanation, especially in the Ottoman context, has been based on the rising borrowing needs of the government.[2]

Although the borrowing needs and high cost of measuring the collector's effort were significant determinants of tax-farming contracts in some cases, our model draws attention to other factors from a broader theoretical perspective. One of these factors was the cost of measuring the tax base. Before a tax-farming contract could be implemented, the government or the tax collector had to measure the tax base to be able to agree (or bid) on the amount of tax-farming contract. Variations in the cost of measuring the tax base explain why, among the tax sources with a high cost of measuring effort, only some were collected by tax-farming contracts and not others. For example, the cost could be lower for large

[2] The borrowing needs of the public sector has been at the core of some explanations of the rise of rent contracts in the Ottoman Empire after the late sixteenth century. See, for example, Darling (1996) and Çızakça (1996). This approach to tax farming has been adopted in most recent narratives of the Ottoman Empire covering this period, such as those by Imber (2002), Johnson and Balla (2009), and Pamuk (2004).

enterprises, such as customs and salt mines with established systems of accounting and record-keeping, than for small ones like blacksmiths and small shops which could require substantial cost to measure their tax base. Even though the cost of monitoring the collector would probably be the same (in proportion to total effort) in both types of enterprises, tax-farming contracts were more likely to be observed in the former than the latter. The difference in the cost of measuring the tax base also explains why tax-farming contracts were more likely in urban than rural sources of tax, all else being the same.

The variance of the tax base was also an important reason why tax-farming contracts were chosen over others in some cases. For example, as noted earlier, tax-farming contracts were more likely to be observed for the collection of customs revenues than excise taxes. The primary reason for this was that the variance of the tax base for customs revenues was likely to be higher in the more volatile environment of international trade than in regional markets because of greater fluctuations in prices, exchange rates, international supply and demand, and political and military stability. Governments preferred tax-farming contracts over share contracts in the collection of customs dues because the collector's effort would be state contingent, giving it an advantage over other types of contracts.

Research on the allocation of tax revenues in the Ottoman Empire provides quantitative support for the importance of variance. For example, a study has found that in the sixteenth century the sources of revenue allocated to local government officials included a higher proportion of variable taxes than those allocated to the provincial and central treasury (Coşgel and Miceli 2005). Clearly, tax bases with a higher proportion of variable taxes would also have a higher variance. Given that wage contracts were observed primarily on provincial and central treasury domains, the result indicates a positive correlation between the variance of the tax base and tax-farming contracts, as predicted by the model.

Changes in the variance of the tax base also explain the rising incidence of tax-farming contracts in the late sixteenth and seventeenth centuries in general. This was generally a period of significant rise in population, inflation, urbanization, and political turmoil around the world. The immediate impact of these changes on tax collection was most likely a significant rise in the variance of tax bases. Whereas governments may have previously preferred to collect some taxes by wage contracts, they now found it more advantageous to switch to tax-farming contracts under the new, more volatile conditions. They did so not necessarily because they became more risk averse or less solvent, but because switching to tax-farming contracts allowed them to maximize the net tax revenue by benefiting from the state-contingent effort associated with this type of contract.

Why Switch to Direct Collection by State Agents

Previous studies have typically attributed the transition from tax farming to salaried state agents to the lower cost of monitoring the tax collectors in strong bureaucracies of modern societies (Kiser 1994). In addition, the model helps us identify other factors that favored the choice of wage contracts by making the alternatives less attractive. One of these factors was the rising costs of measuring the tax base and revenue. Together with urbanization and industrialization, production and exchange was becoming more sophisticated during this period, raising the cost of measuring the value of economic activities that were previously subject to taxes collected under tax-farming contracts. At the same time, a variety of new activities were emerging that needed to be systematically incorporated into the tax system. Because the past was little guide to determining the value of these activities, and because the government, tax collectors, and taxpayers possessed asymmetric information about them, it was costly for the government and the collectors to measure the value of their tax base.

Another factor for some activities was the falling variance of the tax base. Improvements in agricultural technology reduced the risk of crop failure caused by natural disasters, lowering the variance of expected return from these products. Industrialization similarly reduced the effect of natural risks on production and exchange in general. Greater integration of markets reduced the effect of sector-specific influences on revenue, lowering the variance of the tax base. These factors together reduced the value of state-contingent effort that previously made tax-farming contracts beneficial and allowed governments to increase net revenue by switching to wage contracts.

Conclusion

For a theoretical approach to tax farming, we have grouped the rich variety of tax collection methods observed in history into three general categories. Specifically, governments could use share contracts, specifying the proportion at which the two parties would share the tax revenue; tax-farming contracts, where the collector would pay the government a fixed amount based on the value of the tax base; and wage contracts, specifying a fixed wage the government would pay the collector for his or her labor. In explaining the choice among contracts, we have identified the economic cost and benefits of alternative methods of collection that depend on which variables need to be measured—specifically, whether the scheme calls for the government to measure the actual tax collected, the tax base, or the collector's effort—and the value of state-specific collection effort.

Differences in these factors go a long way toward explaining the temporal and spatial use of tax-farming schemes observed in history. These types of contracts became increasingly more common during the sixteenth and seventeenth centuries, notably throughout Europe and the Ottoman Empire, because various demographic and socio-economic changes increased the variance of the tax bases and thus the value of the state-contingent effort associated with this type of contracts. The trend after the seventeenth century was toward greater use of wage contracts in tax collection. A combination of factors, including stronger bureaucracies and more sophisticated production and exchange, increased the cost of measuring the tax base and revenue and lowered the cost of measuring the collectors' effort and the variance of tax bases, making wage contracts increasingly more common and eventually the dominant form of tax collection everywhere.

References

Akdağ, M. (1959). *Türkiyenin İktisadi ve İçtimai Tarihi*. Türk Tarih Kurumu.

Azabou, M. and Nugent, J. B. (1988). Contractual Choice in Tax Collection Activities: Some Implications of the Experience with Tax Farming. *Journal of Institutional and Theoretical Economics* 144, 684–705.

Azabou, M. and Nugent, J. B. (1989). Tax Farming: Anachronism Optimal Contract? (An Illustration with respect to Tunisia's Weekly Markets). In M. K. Nabli and J. Nugent (Eds.), *The New Institutional Economics and Development: Theory and Applications to Tunisia*. North-Holland.

Çizakça, M. (1996). *A Comparative Evolution of Business Partnerships, The Islamic World and Europe, with Specific Reference to the Ottoman Archives*. Brill.

Coşgel, M. M. (2005). Efficiency and Continuity in Public Finance: The Ottoman System of Taxation. *International Journal of Middle East Studies* 37, 567–86.

Coşgel, M. M. and Miceli, T. J. (2005). Risk, Transaction Costs, and Government Finance: The Distribution of Tax Revenue in the Ottoman Empire. *Journal of Economic History* 65, 806–21.

Darling, L. (1996). *Revenue-Raising and Legitimacy: Tax Collection and Finance Administration in the Ottoman Empire, 1560-1660*. Brill.

Imber, C. (2002). *The Ottoman Empire, 1300–1650: The Structure of Power*. Palgrave Macmillan.

Johnson, N. and Balla, E. (2009). "Fiscal crisis and institutional change in the Ottoman Empire and France." *The Journal of Economic History* 69, 809-845.

Kiser, E. (1994). Markets and Hierarchies in Early Modern Tax Systems: A Principal-Agent Analysis. *Politics and Society* 22, 284–315.

Levi, M. (1988). *Of Rule and Revenue*. University of California Press.

Løkkegaard, F. (1950). *Islamic Taxation in the Classic Period, with Special Reference to Circumstances in Iraq*. Branner and Korch.

Pamuk, Ş. (2004). Institutional Change and the Longevity of the Ottoman Empire, 1500-1800. *Journal of Interdisciplinary History* 35, 225–247.

Salzmann, A. C. (1993). An Ancient Regime Revisited: Privatization and Political Economy in the 18th Century Ottoman Empire. *Politics & Society* 21, 393–423.

CHAPTER 8

A Game Theoretical Analysis of Source Allocation in the Early Modern Ottoman Empire Under Contractual Relationships: Case of Thessaloniki Customs

Hande Nur Kırmızıkuşak and Özgür Hakan Aydoğmuş

Substantial scholarly literature on tax collection mechanisms in early modern societies has emerged over the past few decades. This body of work can be examined by using two primary lenses. The first comprises

H. N. Kırmızıkuşak
Faculty of Economics and Administrative Sciences, Yalova University, Yalova, Turkey
e-mail: hande.kirmizikusak@yalova.edu.tr

Ö. H. Aydoğmuş (✉)
Faculty of Political Sciences, Social Sciences University of Ankara, Ankara, Turkey
e-mail: ozgur.aydogmus@asbu.edu.tr

B. Altay (ed.), *Revenue-Raising Institutions, State Organization and Economic Change in the Early Modern Ottoman Empire*, Palgrave Studies in Economic History,
https://doi.org/10.1007/978-3-031-96492-3_8

studies that focus on the historical development of tax collection mechanisms (Ashton 1956; Bonney 1979; Salzmann 1993, 2004; Çizakça 1989, 1996; Darling 1996; Genç 2000; Kwass 2000; White 2004; Vester 2004; Pamuk 2009; Karaman and Pamuk 2010; Drelichman and Voth 2011). This literature predominantly examines the distribution of tax collection rights by rulers to third parties, necessitated by the changing economic environment and high transaction costs of the early modern period. The second stream of the literature concentrates on the efficacy of contracts between rulers and their agents based on tax collection (North and Weingast 1989; Root 1989; Kiser and Schneider 1994; Johnson 2006; Johnson and Koyama 2014; Ma and Rubin 2019; Altay and Oğuz 2021). In this context, analyses are presented by correlating the effectiveness of contracts with the structure of the law and the potential increase in state revenues. Recently, this effectiveness has been examined through the equilibria that have emerged via game theory approaches. The objective of this chapter is to examine the effectiveness of contractual relations in the late sixteenth and early seventeenth centuries by synthesizing historical and theoretical approaches to the Thessaloniki customs—one of the most significant tax-farming contracts of the Ottoman Empire—through a game theoretic approach.

This tax-farming system involved rulers leasing tax sources to private contractors in exchange for a fixed income. The surplus amount exceeding these fixed payments constituted agents' profits. In the first half of the sixteenth century, this tax-farming institution emerged in the Ottoman Empire. From the early periods of the Empire, rulers conducted tax-farming contracts with third parties. However, there were certain structural differences in this institutional organization. These differences were largely attributable to the economic structure and environment. Until the sixteenth century, timar institutions were particularly prevalent in Ottoman tax collection methods. Under this institutional structure, rulers predominantly allocated tax collection rights to military-based groups. Contracts of certain magnitudes were assigned to soldiers who demonstrated achievements in wars according to their ranks. These soldiers were responsible for the productivity and security of the financial resources in their contracts. In return for these responsibilities and military duties, they received a specified portion of the taxes collected as income. The remaining taxes were transferred to the central treasury as state revenue in kind or cash. Within this institutional structure, tax collection rights were distributed to military-based groups according to reputation and rank, rather than auctions. These institutional mechanisms ensured that the Ottoman Empire maintained a ready army, and that its financial structure was sustainable. Consequently, the growth rate of the Ottoman Empire's territorial expansion increased significantly until the end of the sixteenth century.

Since the first decades of the sixteenth century, numerous institutional modifications occurred within this system. The primary factors contributing to these changes were evolving military technologies, the economic milieu, and the imperative to transition to a monetary economy (Genç 2000, p. 102). Concomitantly, the escalating transaction costs associated with the transfer of in-kind tax revenues to the central authority resulting from the expansion of territories constituted a significant factor in institutional transformation. In this sense, the early modern Ottoman Empire exhibited a complex array of institutional arrangements designed to balance the intricate interplay between rulers and their agents. Among these mechanisms, tax farming (*iltizam*) and revenue contracting (*mukataa*) emerged as critical tools for resource allocation and state financing. These arrangements were not merely financial instruments but sophisticated frameworks of negotiation, enforcement, and adaptation that sustained the empire's economic exchanges. This study investigates the Thessaloniki customs system as a case study to investigate how contractual relationships influenced resource allocation and revenue extraction in the Ottoman Empire during the late sixteenth century and the early seventeenth century.

Thessaloniki, a significant port city in the Ottoman Balkans, was a crucial node in the empire's economic network. Its customs functioned as a vital revenue source for the state, while facilitating extensive trade flows with Europe, the Mediterranean, and beyond. However, the administration of customs in Thessaloniki was characterized by considerable complexity. It encompassed a network of interactions among state officials, tax farmers, and merchants, each operating within a framework of incentives and constraints. Analyzing how these stakeholders navigated their roles necessitates a theoretical framework that accounts for strategic decision-making and institutional constraints.

This chapter employs a game-theoretic perspective to analyze resource allocation within the Thessaloniki customs. Game theory provides analytical tools for modeling strategic interactions between the Ottoman state (the principal) and its agents (tax farmers and local elites). Through an examination of these interactions, this study aims to address the following critical questions: How did the Ottoman state design align agents' incentives with its revenue objectives? What mechanisms were implemented to ensure compliance and mitigate the commitment problems?

This study contributes to the broader literature on Ottoman economic history and institutional development by providing a novel perspective on governance and resource allocation dynamics. Through the integration of game theory with historical evidence, it seeks to elucidate the mechanisms that sustained the Thessaloniki customs, while illuminating the challenges of pre-modern economic governance. The findings also offer comparative insights into the institutional trajectories of other pre-modern empires such as those in Western Europe and China, emphasizing the interplay between agents and rulers in shaping economic outcomes under the tax-farming institution of the Ottoman Empire.

Historical and Theoretical Background: Historical Analysis and Game Theory

From the early decades of the sixteenth century, the Ottoman Empire's fiscal revenues relied predominantly on contractual arrangements, particularly through tax-farming contracts (İnalcık 2000, p. 105). These systems were implemented to decentralize revenue collection, while maintaining a consistent flow of income to the central treasury. Under the tax-farming institution, individuals or groups submitted bids for the right to collect taxes from specific revenue sources, including customs duties. Successful bidders, designated tax farmers, were obligated to deliver fixed revenue to the state while retaining any surplus profit. In studies of Ottoman budgets, there were no estimates of the share of revenues from tax-farming contracts in the budget until the mid-seventeenth century. However, one estimate determined the long-term proportions of contract revenues in the budget from the latter half of the seventeenth century to the final quarter of the seventeenth century (Çakır 2006). Although this long-term estimate did not encompass the study period, it provided significant findings on the importance of tax-farming contracts in Ottoman fiscal revenues.

Figure 8.1 illustrates the long-term perspective of the proportion of revenue collected by tax farmers and state officials in the state revenues. An examination of Fig. 8.1 reveals three primary patterns. The first encompasses the second half of the seventeenth century. The proportion of revenue obtained from tax-farming contracts in the budget is significantly higher than that collected by state officials. In the second pattern, this trend has shifted for the period that covers last years of the seventeenth century. This change appears in favor of taxes collected by state officials. The third pattern indicates that revenues obtained from tax-farming contracts began to constitute a relatively higher share in the budget from the second half of the seventeenth century onward. However, this change does not indicate a significant difference as much as the first pattern in terms of the shares of tax collection methods in state revenues. What factors contribute to the apparently higher proportion of revenue collected through tax-farming contracts? Why did this pattern substantially reverse in the subsequent periods? Although the share of revenues obtained from tax-farming contracts increased from the second half of the seventeenth century onward, why did this situation not result in a substantial premium between different tax collection methods, as observed in the second half of the seventeenth century?

In the first pattern in Fig. 8.1, the proportion of tax-farming revenues in budgets in the mid-seventeenth century was approximately 70%. This rate is also indicative of the previous periods. It is probable that the majority of the tax resources were allocated to tax farmers until this period. However, this process provides limited insights into the efficacy

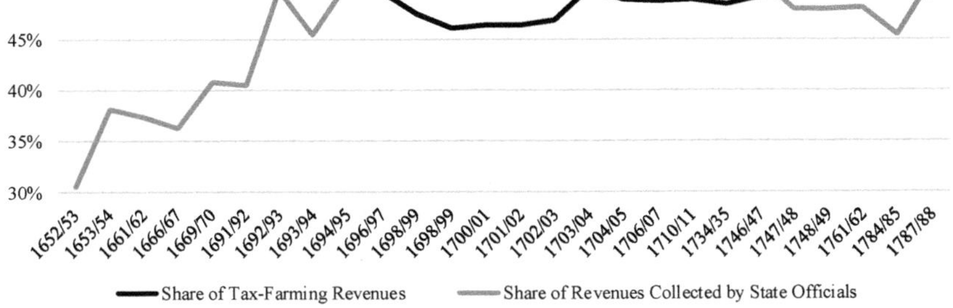

Fig. 8.1 Long-term proportions of revenues collected by tax farmers and state officials in budgets (*Note* Çakır 2006: 184–85)

of institutional mechanisms. Ariel Salzmann (1993) argues that it was a natural progression for the Ottoman Empire to transition from timar contracts to tax-farming contracts, given the expanding geography of the empire. Indeed, the high transaction costs associated with expanding territories, increasing costs of monitoring mechanisms, and information costs should compel rulers to redirect risks to tax farmers (Coşgel and Miceli 2005, 2009). The demand for tax-farming contracts has continued to increase and the majority of taxes began to be collected by private entities. However, a significant indicator of institutional effectiveness relates to commitment problems (Balla and Johnson 2009; Altay and Oğuz 2021). An estimate suggests that the commitment problem that emerged in tax-farming contracts until the first half of the seventeenth century was relatively less severe than that in subsequent periods (Altay and Oğuz 2021, p. 80). It can be argued that although the substantial depreciation of Ottoman currencies in 1585 and subsequent Jelali rebellions created an insecure environment, the commitment problem remained minimal until the late seventeenth century. In other words, the discrepancies between the intended and actual durations of contracts signed by rulers and their agents remain relatively small. This situation explains why, in addition to the increasing cash income requirements, a significant portion of tax revenue was collected through tax-farming contracts in the second half of the seventeenth century.

The pattern that emerged in the first half of the eighteenth century differed significantly from the initial pattern. Although the demand for tax-farming contracts increased during this period, their proportion of budget revenues declined below that of state officials (Fig. 8.1). This situation arose during the institutional change period. The decrease in the proportion of tax-farming contracts, particularly from the second half of the seventeenth century onward, precipitated this institutional change. Under this institutional structure, rulers allocate short-term contracts to tax farmers. These short-term contracts resulted in contracts changing hands, especially during periods of heightened uncertainty such as war, drought, natural disasters, and changes in rulers. Consequently, contracts that were already short term in nature changed hands more rapidly, reducing the incentive for taxed farmers to invest. In this case, the productivity of the tax source diminishes over time because of the motivation to earn short-term income and lack of long-term investment (Genç 2000, p. 107). As a result, the proportion of tax sources in the budget revenue decreases. However, it would be erroneous to attribute the decrease in the proportion of tax-farming contracts in budget revenues solely to the commitment problem or absence of corporate bodies. As mentioned, external shocks beyond control may have more substantial effects on short-term contracts. For instance, why did the proportion of income from tax-farming contracts decrease toward the end of the century, when it was relatively high in the middle of the seventeenth century? Whether the emergence of a commitment problem or the absence of a corporate body among tax farmers could have had a substantial effect in such a brief period is a significant question for discussion.

The institutional transformation that emerged in the second pattern coincides with the conversion of tax-farming contracts into long-term agreements. While Ottoman rulers transferred the contracts to tax farmers on a lifelong basis, they also extended the opportunity for the heirs of these groups to continue the contracts. The primary objective of this study was to enhance the productivity of tax resources through long-term contracts. These extended agreements were intended to incentivize tax farmers to invest and provide a new source of revenue for the budget through advance payments, which constituted a novel requirement for obtaining these contracts. The advance payment (*muaccele*) required for long-term contracts was approximately 10–12 times the annual payment. In addition to this advance payment, tax farmers would continue their annual remittances. While it was anticipated that the initiation of advance payments and the emergence of long-term contracts would increase the proportion of tax-farming contracts in budget revenues, it was observed that the share of jizya and *avarız* (extraordinary) taxes collected by state officials increased significantly (Fig. 8.1). This increase was not indicative of a deficiency in the new institutional organization, but rather was associated with the partial development of the bureaucratic structure during this period. The budget revenue trends presented subsequently provide empirical evidence of this phenomenon.

In the second half of the eighteenth century, when the third pattern emerged, a distinct structure developed from the previous period owing to the influence of long-term tax-farming contracts. The proportion of tax-farming revenue surpassed that of other tax collection methods. However, the relative difference between the two tax collection methods was not as substantial as in the second half of the seventeenth century. A significant factor contributing to this could be the decrease in tax-farming contract revenues due to the uncertainty generated by Russian wars that arose, particularly in the second half of the eighteenth century.

Nevertheless, what is frequently emphasized in Ottoman literature is the increase in the influence of local groups (Pamuk 2000, p. 110). The acquisition of contracts by these groups and the weakening of monitoring mechanisms resulted in revenue being concentrated in the hands of local entities. The practice of these groups borrowing from wealthy individuals and presenting them as guarantors to obtain contracts led to a reduction in the Ottoman center's share of revenues (Çizakça 1996, p. 166). Consequently, although revenue from tax-farming contracts increased, the fact that they began to be transferred to the central treasury at a lower rate was one of the primary reasons for the third pattern. It is probable that the transfer of some taxes collected by state officials to local groups under contracts increased the proportion of tax-farming revenues. During this period, the commitment problem intensified and the discrepancies between the intended and actual durations of contracts began to widen. According to one estimate, this increase was at least 5–6 times compared to the second half of the seventeenth century (Altay and Oğuz 2021, p. 80).

Figure 8.2 illustrates the long-term trajectory of Ottoman budget revenues from the latter half of the seventeenth century to the final period of the eighteenth century. While the proportions of tax revenues collected through various methods in budgets exhibit significant discontinuities, Ottoman revenues demonstrate an increasing trend over the long term. Notably, in the early eighteenth century, when the proportion of tax-farming revenues began to decline and in the latter half, when commitment issues were presumed to intensify, budget revenues exhibit a more pronounced increase. These indicators, derived from primary sources, present findings that contradict hypotheses based on commitment issues or institutional deficiencies. A pertinent inquiry is whether these revenues could have increased further if the existing commitment issues had been minimized and tax farmers had succeeded in establishing institutional bodies, as observed in France. It is challenging to estimate the optimal level of tax revenue for a state encompassing a vast geographical area such as the Ottoman Empire. It is also difficult to assert that the taxes collected are at an optimal level. In particular, since the latter half of the eighteenth century, the emergence of local elites has further complicated claims of revenue optimization. It can be argued that the Ottoman Empire managed to increase its tax revenue within prevailing institutional, political, and economic structures (Salzmann 1993). Considering its geographical expansion, the absence of structures similar to those in France, England, and even Prussia may not necessarily indicate a deficiency but rather may have been perceived as a costly solution for the state. Employing diverse methodologies to analyze these historically presented findings has the potential to provide new insights and contributions regarding how the Ottoman Empire succeeded in increasing its revenues through methods distinct from those of other states.

Auction of tax-farming rights is a critical mechanism for resource allocation. This mechanism has two primary purposes: First, it enables the state to extract information regarding the expected value of revenue sources as bidders reveal their estimates through their offers. Second, it establishes a competitive environment that incentivizes tax farmers to bid aggressively, thereby maximizing the state's immediate revenue. However, this system also introduces risks because overbidding may lead to defaults, and the state must navigate the trade-off between maximizing short-term income and ensuring long-term stability. Contracts in the Ottoman tax-farming system were not static but were subject to renegotiation and renewal. Periodic renegotiation allowed the state to adapt to changing economic and political conditions such as fluctuations in trade volumes or external shocks such as wars. While this flexibility was beneficial, it also introduced uncertainties for tax farmers, who had to account for the

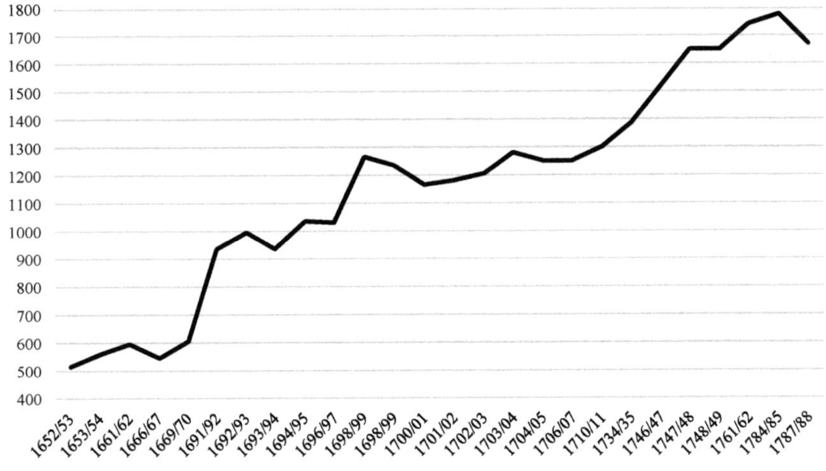

Fig. 8.2 State revenues, 1652–1788 (in millions, akçe) (*Note* Çakır 2006: 184)

possibility of unfavorable changes. Additionally, the state employed monitoring mechanisms, such as audits and the use of local officials, to ensure compliance and mitigate the risk of fraud or shirking.

The contractual nature of revenue collection in the Ottoman Empire elucidates the interplay between formal agreements and informal practices. While contracts delineate the obligations of tax farmers, enforcement frequently relies on informal trust and mutual dependence networks. These networks are particularly significant in regions such as Thessaloniki, where the involvement of local elites and merchants plays a crucial role in ensuring efficient functioning of the contracts.

Game theory provides a systematic framework for analyzing strategic interactions that characterize resource allocation and governance in historical institutions (Greif 2002). In the Ottoman Empire, the administration of revenue-generating systems such as Thessaloniki customs encompassed a complex network of relationships among the state, tax farmers, and merchants. Each of these entities pursued their own interests within the constraints imposed by the institutional environment, resulting in a dynamic interplay between incentives and strategies. Game theory is particularly efficacious for examining these interactions as it elucidates the underlying logic that shapes decisions and outcomes.

The principal-agent problem provides a valuable analytical framework for examining the relationship between the Ottoman state and its agents, specifically tax farmers (Kiser 1994). In this context, the state, acting as the principal, delegated the responsibility for revenue collection to tax farmers, who served as agents tasked with maximizing revenue while fulfilling a predetermined quota to the state. However, the inherent information and power asymmetry between the two parties presents significant challenges. The state's limited ability to fully monitor agents' activities creates opportunities for potential malfeasance, corruption, and inefficiency. Conversely, tax farmers faced uncertainties regarding state behavior, including the risk of arbitrary asset seizures or unilateral renegotiation of terms.

The commitment problem constituted another critical issue, as neither party could fully trust the other in honor agreements in the absence of credible enforcement mechanisms. The state required assurance that tax farmers would fulfill their contractual obligations, while tax farmers necessitated guarantees that the state would respect their profits and rights. These concerns frequently necessitated the development of sophisticated contracts and utilization of third-party enforcement mechanisms, such as local elites or judicial institutions, to mitigate the risk of defection.

Game theory also emphasizes the concept of Nash equilibrium, in which players select strategies that are optimal, given the strategies chosen by others. In the context of the Thessaloniki customs, equilibrium outcomes reflect the balance of power and incentives among the state, tax farmers, and merchants. For instance, tax farmers' decisions regarding the level of effort to invest in efficient revenue collection were contingent on their expectations about the state's willingness to enforce contracts and merchants' compliance with tax obligations. An analysis of these equilibria facilitates an explanation of both the stability and fragility of the Ottoman revenue mechanisms under various conditions. Through the application of game theory to the Thessaloniki customs, this study offers a nuanced analysis of how the Ottoman Empire navigated the complexities of resource allocation and institutional governance. Furthermore, it elucidates the broader implications of these findings for the examination of pre-modern economic systems and the influence of strategic behavior in shaping historical outcomes.

Context, Data, and Limitations: Contract Prices and Durations of the Thessaloniki Customs

This study uses tax-farming contracts pertaining to the Thessaloniki customs. The study dataset comprises 14 consecutive contracts spanning the period from 1591 to 1619. These contracts are currently housed in the Maliyeden Müdevver Defterler (MAD) within the State Archives of the Presidency of the Republic of Türkiye (BOA). These registers contain tax-farming contracts only sporadically. Therefore, this study references a pioneering study that serves as a reliable secondary source and examines the competitiveness of the tax-farming contracts employed in the Ottoman Empire (Çizakça 1993). This study presents a comprehensive view of the Thessaloniki customs over a specific period. This dataset, derived from primary sources, presents variables associated with contracts in their raw form. Specifically, the prices and annual payment amounts of contracts are nominal. To address this limitation, monetary values were initially calculated in real terms using the Istanbul Consumer Price Index (ICPI) within the scope of this study (Özmucur and Pamuk 2002). Real values facilitate more accurate assumptions to reveal the changes and challenges that occur in contracts. Another significant limitation of these sources is that contracts are recorded in a dispersed manner within a vast archive without sequential organization. Moreover, when these contracts fail to attract buyers during certain periods, the central authority collects taxes on these resources through state officials. The difficulty of tracking these situations from the archive impedes the creation of a long-term series. Consequently, the analyses yield only short-term findings, and the general applicability of the assumptions derived from these findings is limited. Given these constraints, this study analyzes the processes by which tax-farming contracts changed hands in the Ottoman Empire, using a game theoretic approach. However, prior to applying this approach, it would be beneficial to include a descriptive analysis of the socioeconomic structure of the city of Thessaloniki and the customs contracts.

Thessaloniki had played a significant role in the social and economic structure of the Ottoman Empire for a long period. First, the city accommodated various groups from diverse societies. From the late fifteenth century to the end of the nineteenth century, the ratio of Muslims to non-Muslims in the city of Thessaloniki remained approximately equal (Kiel 2009, pp. 352–357). This diversity in demographic composition also played a determining role in the economic structure of the city and contributed to an increase in trade. Concurrently, the city's proximity to the sea enhances the value of its ports. In the latter half of the eighteenth century, imports, particularly from Egypt, played a substantial role in the city's economic structure (Greene 2000, p. 130). Thessaloniki became an important trade network, especially in raisin-commerce (Greene 2000, p. 140). The city also played a significant role in textile production and trade. Jews who migrated to Thessaloniki in the late fifteenth century specialized in woolen cloth production (Faroqhi 2004, p. 148). Furthermore, Thessaloniki had a considerable number of cash waqfs. These organizations, which functioned as financial institutions prior to modern banks, operated as credit institutions. The concentration of these organizations in this city, particularly from the first half of the eighteenth century, and their provision of substantial financial resources, provided insights into Thessaloniki's economic importance and development (Aydın 2014). Moreover, there were various tax-farming contracts in Thessaloniki in addition to customs. In this city, significant contracts in diverse economic sectors, notably in the production of candles, dye, salt, valonia tree, wine, coffee, and wool, were allocated to tax farmers through auctions (Çizakça 1993, pp. 236–250). In summary, the city's diverse demographic composition and multifaceted economic production provided significant insights into the relevance of customs contracts.

Figure 8.3 illustrates the progression of auction prices and annual payments for the Thessaloniki customs. As previously mentioned, the data presented are derived from 14 auctions. An initial examination of Fig. 8.3 reveals two primary patterns. The first is characterized by a relatively stable auction price trajectory between 1591 and 1607. The figure demonstrates that contracts remain under the management of tax farmers for brief periods due to various factors. Within the first pattern, a decrease in the prices offered for customs is observed in 1596. This reduction can be attributed to the inability of previous tax farmers to fulfill the bid price, resulting in a more realistic price being proposed by a different tax farmer during the reauction. However, a closer analysis of 1596 indicates that the contract changed ownership twice more within the same year, with prices increasing during this period. Although the contract price rises to 2.11 million akçe in the final bid of 1596, this figure remained below the 2.37 million akçe offered two years prior. In auctions up to 1607, the contract price exhibits an upward trend. However, these increases occur at modest rates. The price established in the 1607 auction merely reaches the level of 1591. The modest fluctuations in the first pattern can be attributed to initial prices being set at unsustainably high levels. However, the subsequent increasing trend in prices is a result of different tax farmers raising their bids and securing the right to collect taxes. It is evident that tax farmers who proposed higher prices obtained the right to collect taxes at the time of their offer, leading to the premature termination of existing contracts.

The second pattern occurred over a shorter period between 1613 and 1619. During this brief interval, the contracts pertaining to the Thessaloniki customs changed ownership six times, accompanied by more substantial fluctuations in auction prices compared to the previous pattern. While prices increased rapidly during this period, the subsequent decrease was equally precipitous. The significant increase in auction prices could be largely attributed to competition among tax farmers. Conversely, the decreases stem from the reduced sustainability of contracts due to high auction prices. In 1613, the contract prices reached approximately 5.5 million akçe, while a subsequent bid in the same year elevated this price by nearly 35% to 7.5 million akçe. Although the tax farmer who acquired the contract at the highest price maintained it for three years, in 1616, the Thessaloniki customs were transferred to another tax farmer via

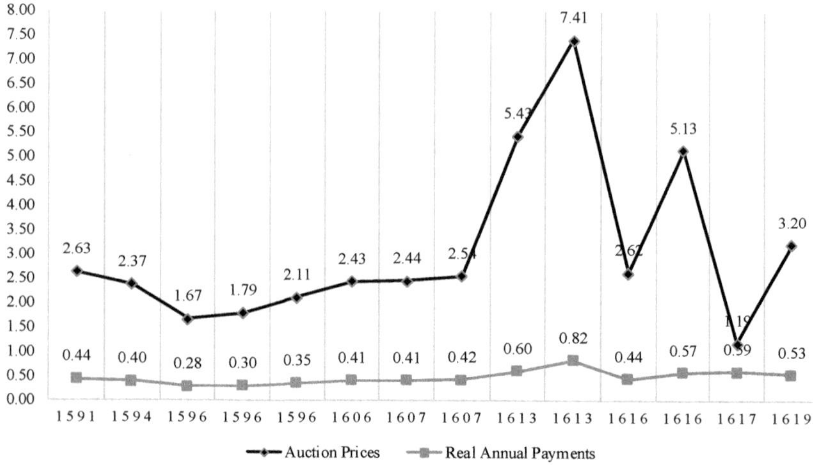

Fig. 8.3 Trend of auction prices and annual payments of the Thessaloniki customs (in millions of akçe) (*Note* This data is derived from Çizakça (1993))

auction, presumably due to payment difficulties. While the initial auction price in 1616 was 2.62 million akçe, a different tax farmer subsequently acquired the contract with a bid of 5.13 million akçe in the same year. In the second pattern, there were substantial decreases in the auction prices of the contracts in the final two auctions compared to previous years, and in 1619, a different tax farmer was awarded the contract for 3.2 million akçe.

Although significant fluctuations in auction prices are observed, a primary contributing factor is the duration of the contracts. Specifically, longer contract periods correlate with higher prices requested in the auction. For more precise evaluations, the annual payments of the Thessaloniki customs following each auction are also presented in real terms in akçe (Fig. 8.3). Upon initial examination, the trajectory of annual payments appears more horizontal and stable. The annual payments, calculated by dividing the auction prices by the respective contract years, remain relatively consistent between 1591 and 1607. However, in 1613, the annual payment amounts for the Thessaloniki customs initially increase to 0.6 million akçe and subsequently to 0.82 million akçe. Nevertheless, following a decrease in 1616, the annual payments stabilize once again, reaching 0.53 million akçe in 1619. When analyzed over an extended period, the annual income of the Thessaloniki customs to the state treasury in real terms increased by only 20% during this timeframe.

Figure 8.4 shows the long-term course of the intended and the actual durations contracts. As can be seen, the duration determined by the central authority for all contracts between 1591 and 1607 was six years. While these durations increased to nine years between 1613 and 1616, they were auctioned for two years, with a significant decrease in 1617. The contract that was finally given in 1619 was reauctioned for six years. The auction prices of the contracts were determined according to the intended duration. The examinations made according to the annual payments provided more accurate results when examining the income expected from the Thessaloniki customs. For example, the large decrease in the auction price in 1617 was because this contract was to be given for two years. However, when the annual payment was considered, the intended duration of the contract did not seem to have a significant effect. The data presented in Fig. 8.4 and the long-term course provided another dimension. There was a significant difference between the intended and actual durations determined for contracts in auctions. This difference theoretically indicated a commitment problem. In this sample, the intended and actual durations of the contracts given only in 1607 and 1617 were equal. In other words, tax farmers who received the contract managed to protect their tax collection rights until the end of the contract. During other periods, a serious commitment problem appeared. However, it would be important to examine whether this commitment problem causes a loss in tax revenue.

When the Thessaloniki customs are considered from this perspective, the central treasury earned approximately 16.04 million akçe in revenue between 1591 and 1619, thanks to the competitive structure created by the auctions and the fact that the higher bidder took the contract at the time of the bid. However, if the first bid in 1591 had been protected by the terms of the contract for these 30 years, the state treasury's revenue would have been approximately 13.14 million akçe. This situation necessitates an analytical examination of the tax-farming contracts that emerged in the Ottoman Empire from different perspectives. An analytical examination of the long-term effectiveness of these contracts, especially those based on auctions, negotiations, and bargaining, provides concrete clues for understanding the effectiveness of the in-situation structure. Even if there was a commitment problem, the income of the state obtained from the Thessaloniki customs increased over this short period. Here, it

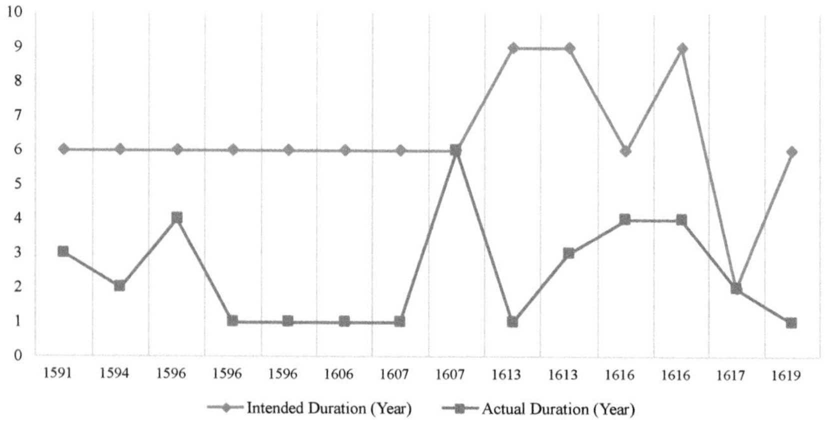

Fig. 8.4 The long-term relationship between intended and actual durations (*Note* This data is derived from Çizakça (1993))

seems that the state managed to protect its income through the contracts it redistributed through negotiations. In fact, with a slightly higher offer, the state might have earned significantly more than it did by awarding the contract under the terms of 1591. From this perspective, it would not be wrong to assume that Ottoman rulers wanted to increase their income by creating a commitment problem through auctions. It can also be suggested that Ottoman rulers assumed a certain amount of risk through these commitment problems and took short-term decreases in annual payments caused by the commitment problem. However, evaluating these assumptions through the game theoretic approach is important in terms of understanding long-term equilibrium(s) and choices of contracting parties to examine institutional effectiveness under contractual relations.

A Game Theoretical Approach to Tax-Farming Contracts

Here we propose a game theoretic model for tax-farming contracts in the Thessalonica customs. As mentioned above, the land including crop fields, mines, and customs belong to the central government and the government rents these properties to elites of the region. In the case of customs, these elites are called tax farmers. When considering a tax-farming contract, one needs to consider two main players namely the ruler or the state and the tax farmers. The game form presented here is based on a Prisoner's Dilemma Game and its characteristics (Gintis 2009, p. 50–51).

The tax farmers agree to pay a predetermined fixed amount, and the surplus amount exceeding these fixed payments constitute the tax farmer's profits. Tax farmers may exploit this contract by overcharging duties (such as inflated rates, unnecessary fees, or manipulating valuations) or deliberate obstruction (like delaying the release of goods or conducting excessive and costly inspections).

The ruler, on the other hand, may choose to honor or break the contract. In the case of the Thessalonica customs, only 2 of 14 contracts were honored by the ruler in between 1591 and 1619.

First, suppose the common belief about the government's behavior is that the ruler honors contacts.

If the tax farmer does not exploit, then let the ruler's and tax farmer's respective payoffs be a and α. On the other hand, if tax farmer exploits, they obtain b and β where $a > b$ and $\alpha < \beta$. In the case of exploitation, the tax farmer gets more because of overcharging duties or deliberate obstruction. In this case, the ruler gets less since exploitation can discourage trade and reduce long-term revenue from customs and other taxes.

Now let us consider the case that the ruler does not honor contacts in general. When the tax farmer does not exploit, let the payoffs of the ruler and tax farmer be c and γ. In this case ruler's payoff increases, i.e. $c > a$ since it enables competition in the market using bids more often and gets no harm from exploitation. If, on the other hand, tax farmer exploits than let their respective payoffs be d and δ. In this case, exploitation will be more beneficial for the tax farmer and hence $\delta > \gamma$.

To identify the relationship between b and d consider the following. Suppose the tax farmer exploits then honoring the contract rather than breaking it will be more costly for the government and hence $b < d$.

With these assumptions, we have the bimatrix game given in Fig. 8.5.

To analyze the game we will use above-given inequalities. Recall whether the tax farmer plays exploit or not exploit, for the ruler it is always better to break the contract. This follows from the inequalities $c > a$ and $b < d$. This is to say that the government's payoff increases when the ruler chooses to break the contract whether the tax farmer exploits or not.

Fig. 8.5 Payoff matrix

Ruler/Tax Farmer	not exploit	exploit
honor the contract	(a, α)	(b, β)
break the contract	(c, γ)	(d, δ)

Similarly, the tax farmers payoff always increases when choosing to exploit. This fact follows from the inequalities $\alpha < \beta$ and $\delta > \gamma$. As a result, when playing the Nash equilibrium for the above-given game, the ruler chooses breaking the contract and the tax farmer chooses exploiting.

To determine Pareto optimal outcome, we must compare the outcomes (a, α) and (d, δ). The first outcome represents a stable situation in which both actors do not cheat, ensuring mutual trust and sustained cooperation. The second outcome corresponds to a case in which the ruler breaches the contract by terminating it earlier than the agreed date, destabilizing the relationship and undermining trust and tax farmers exploit the custom for their benefit.

This analysis ties directly to the institutional transformation introduced by the Ottoman malikâne system, which converted short-term tax-farming arrangements into long-term contracts. By offering tax farming on a lifelong basis with inheritable rights, the Ottoman rulers aimed to create stability and align incentives between the state and tax farmers. The lifelong contracts represented an attempt to move toward outcomes resembling (a, α), where mutual cooperation minimizes the risk of exploitation or breach. Hence the ruler class agrees on the idea that the more stable outcome (a, α) is more beneficial for the government in the long run, i.e. $a > d$. The ruler class could also reduce the payoff of tax farmers if they choose to exploit, and early termination of the contract is not the only way of doing this. By securing long-term agreements and extending them to heirs, the system was expected to create a more predictable and stable framework for tax collection, encouraging investment and reducing the incentives for either party to deviate from cooperative behavior.

In conclusion, the transition to long-term contracts like those under the malikâne system can be seen as an institutional solution to ensure outcomes closer to Pareto optimality, fostering trust and reducing conflicts between rulers and tax farmers.

An Assessment Over Historical Case and Game Theoretical Perspective

The Ottoman tax-farming system during the early modern period provided an intriguing case study of institutional dynamics and economic efficiency. Centered on auctions and redistributive contracts, the system allowed the state to maximize short-term revenues but at the expense of long-term stability. Analyzing the revenue generated by the Thessaloniki customs between 1591 and 1619 demonstrates the dual-edged nature of this approach. While competitive bidding led to higher immediate earnings, the frequent breaches of contracts by the state created systemic inefficiencies. A game theoretical approach reveals how commitment problems were inherent in this structure and sheds light on the broader implications for institutional development.

This assessment evaluates the inefficiencies of the Ottoman tax-farming system, examines its historical paradox in which commitment problem provided higher economic returns, and analyzes potential solutions to commitment problems. The focus on the Thessaloniki customs provides a nuanced understanding of the balance between short-term fiscal gains and the necessity of long-term institutional stability.

Thessaloniki's customs provided a comprehensive case study to examine the mechanisms of Ottoman tax farming. Between 1591 and 1619, the central treasury accrued approximately 16.04 million akçe. This outcome was primarily attributed to the competitive nature of auctions, wherein contracts were awarded to the highest bidder. Had the initial bid from 1591 been maintained for the entire 30-year period, the state would have garnered only approximately 13.14 million akçe. Consequently, redistributive auctions appeared to be a financially advantageous strategy.

The findings derived from the 30-year short-term examination of the tax-farming contracts of the Thessaloniki customs substantiate the hypothesis that short-term contracts and auctions are more efficacious (Salzmann 1993). The elevated transportation and monitoring costs, coupled with the extensive geography of the empire, compel the institutional structure toward short-term and auction-based contracts, elucidating the emergence of tax collection institutions in this manner.

The hierarchical collection of tax collection rights through bureaucratic methods necessitates the state's assumption of certain risks and impedes state officials from conducting more effective monitoring owing to high costs (Coşgel and Miceli 2009). Consequently, the risk is entirely transferred to tax farmers, and the collection of taxes, executed through frequent auctions, results in higher tax collection in the Thessaloniki customs. In essence, the state augments its revenues in the long term (30 years for these contracts) by accommodating short-term decreases in annual revenue. It is seen that had the contract been awarded to the tax farmer who made the initial offer in 1591, and this tax farmer had maintained fixed annual payments arising from this offer, revenues would have been lower. The paradox that emerges pertains to the sustainability of income obtained from the commitment problem created through auctions. Figure 8.1 shows that since the late of the seventeenth century, the income obtained through tax-farming contracts fell below that collected by state officials.

However, this revenue maximization came at a significant cost. Of the 14 contracts during this period, only two were fully honored by the state. This contract breach pattern undermined trust and stability. Tax farmers who were cognizant of the likelihood of premature contract termination were incentivized to exploit their positions (Genç 2000, p. 107). Overcharging duties, imposing superfluous fees, and delaying shipments became the prevalent practices. These actions discouraged trade and reduced the long-term revenue potential of customs, illustrating the inefficiency of the system. The state's strategy of redistributing contracts through competitive bidding reflected the prioritization of short-term revenue generation. This approach also revealed a fundamental commitment problem: the state lacked the capacity to credibly commit to honoring contracts, while tax farmers could not be relied upon to abstain from exploitative practices.

The dynamics of the Ottoman tax-farming system can be conceptualized as a game theoretic model involving two primary actors: the ruler (state) and tax farmers. The state possesses two strategic options, honoring or breaching contracts, while tax farmers can either exploit or refrain from exploiting their positions. The payoffs for each party were contingent on these choices, and the Nash equilibrium revealed the inherent inefficiency of the system. When the ruler honored contracts and tax farmers abstained from exploitation, the system achieved a stable outcome, albeit infrequent. In this scenario, mutual trust ensured long-term benefits for both parties. However, when tax farmers exploited their positions, the ruler experienced diminished revenue and was incentivized to breach the contract. Conversely, if the ruler consistently breached contracts, tax farmers anticipated instability and increased exploitative behavior. Frequent breaches of contracts by the state demonstrate that they often prioritize short-term gains over long-term stability. Similarly, tax farmers consistently opted for exploitation, as their payoffs from over-charging or obstructing trade exceeded those from cooperative behavior. This interaction results in a Nash equilibrium, wherein both parties act in self-interest, leading to a Pareto-inefficient outcome.

The Ottoman experience contrasts markedly with institutional developments in Western Europe, where robust property rights and representative institutions have facilitated more cooperative arrangements between states and economic actors (Balla and Johnson 2009). The inefficiencies of the Ottoman system were rooted in the centralized and patrimonial nature of its governance. Unlike Western European states, which developed legal frameworks to enforce contracts and protect property rights, the Ottoman Empire relied on the informal mechanisms of trust and reputation. This reliance limited the scope of institutional innovation and exacerbated commitment problems.

The absence of representative institutions played a critical role in this process. In Western Europe, bodies such as parliaments functioned as mediators between rulers and economic elites, enforcing agreements and reducing the likelihood of breaches. In contrast, the Ottoman state's centralized structure concentrated authority on the hands of the ruler, leaving little room for independent enforcement mechanisms. This lack of checks and balances facilitated the state's ability to breach contracts when fiscal pressures arose. Economic factors also contributed to these differences. While Western Europe's growing urban centers and commercial economies necessitated institutional stability, the predominantly agrarian Ottoman economy did not exert similar pressures. The economic elites in the Ottoman Empire were primarily landowners and tax farmers who lacked the collective bargaining power of merchant and capitalist classes in Europe.

The commitment problems inherent in the Ottoman tax-farming system stem from a lack of credible enforcement mechanisms and the state's time-inconsistent preferences. Several potential solutions to these problems can be derived from institutional theory and historical practice.

One solution involved the transition to the Malikâne system, which introduced long-term inheritable tax-farming contracts (Pamuk 2009, p. 22). By offering tax farmers more secure rights, the system sought to align their incentives with those of the state. Tax farmers were more likely to invest in infrastructure and administrative improvements, knowing that their rights would be protected. This approach provides a more stable and predictable revenue stream to the state. However, the Malikâne system is challenging. Its reliance on elite networks sometimes reinforced inequalities, and the state retained its ultimate authority, which could undermine trust. One estime indicates increasing gap between intended and actual durations in malikane contracts (Altay and Oğuz 2021, p. 80). Although the state revenues show an increasing pattern as shown in Fig. 8.2, the expectations on increasing investment and productivity remain limited during the eighteenth century (Genç 2000, p. 115; Pamuk 2009, 23). Another potential solution is to develop independent enforcement mechanisms. By codifying contracts and establishing judicial bodies to oversee disputes, the state could have reduced the uncertainty surrounding tax-farming agreements. These mechanisms would have provided credible commitment to both parties, encouraging cooperative behavior as emerged in England following the Glorious Revolution, for instance (North and Weingast 1989; North et al. 2009).

The inefficiencies of the Ottoman tax-farming system elucidate the challenges of balancing short-term fiscal requirements with long-term institutional stability. The state's dependence on redistributive contracts maximizes immediate revenue; however, it undermines trust and cooperation, resulting in Pareto-inefficient outcomes. The transition to the Malikâne system represents a significant attempt to address these challenges; however, it was not a comprehensive solution. The disparities between Ottoman experience and Western Europe underscore the significance of representative institutions and independent enforcement mechanisms in addressing commitment problems. While the Ottoman Empire's centralized governance limited the scope of institutional innovation, its reforms demonstrated an ongoing effort to adapt to changing economic and political realities. An analysis of these dynamics provides valuable insights into the broader challenges of institutional development and economic governance in the pre-modern states.

Conclusion

This analysis of the Ottoman tax-farming system, particularly the case of the Thessaloniki customs, offers critical insights into the dynamics of institutional design, economic governance, and the pervasive challenges of commitment problems in pre-modern states. Through the application of a game-theoretical framework, it elucidates the tension between short-term fiscal strategies and the necessity for long-term stability, a recurring dilemma in centralized systems such as the Ottoman Empire. An examination of tax-farming contracts demonstrates how trust, incentives, and enforcement mechanisms can shape economic outcomes, providing a more comprehensive understanding of why certain institutional arrangements lead to inefficiency.

The significance of this analysis lies in its capacity to bridge historical inquiry with theoretical models, elucidating how institutional evolution responds to both internal dynamics and external pressure. By examining Ottoman states' reliance on redistributive auctions and their subsequent transition to long-term contracts under the Malikâne system, this study provides a nuanced perspective on the interplay between state authority and economic agents. This underscores the risks of time-inconsistent behavior and the potential for reforms that align incentives between rulers and economic actors.

For future studies, this analysis offers a robust framework to explore similar institutional challenges in other historical and regional contexts. The game theoretical approach provides a replicable model for examining the consequences of commitment problems across diverse governance systems, enabling comparisons with Western Europe, China, and other pre-modern economies. Furthermore, it invites interdisciplinary research combining economic history with political science and legal studies to foster a comprehensive understanding of institutional development.

This study has practical implications for contemporary governance. The historical lessons derived from the Ottoman tax-farming system can inform modern policy debates on contract enforcement, property rights, and the state's role in economic regulation. By elucidating how institutional arrangements can either mitigate or exacerbate inefficiencies, policymakers and scholars can design systems that balance short-term and long-term stability. Thus, this analysis serves as both a historical case study and a foundation for broader theoretical and practical investigations of institutional effectiveness.

References

Altay, B. and Oğuz, F. (2021). *Rules, Contracts and Law Enforcement in the Ottoman Empire: The Case of Tax-Farming Contracts*. Palgrave Macmillan.

Ashton, R. (1956). Revenue Farming under the Early Stuarts. *The Economic History Review* 8(3), 310–322.

Aydın, H. V. (2014). Selanik'te 18. Yüzyılın İlk Yarısında Para Vakıfları ve Kredi İşlemleri. *Tarih İncelemeleri Dergisi* 29(1), 87–106.

Balla, E. and Johnson, N. D. (2009). Fiscal Crisis and Institutional Change in the Ottoman Empire and France. *The Journal of Economic History* 69(3), 809–845.

Bonney, R. J. (1979). The Failure of French Revenue Farms, 1600-60. *The Economic History Review* 32(1), 11–32.

Coşgel, M. and Miceli, T. (2005). Risk, Transaction Costs, and Government Finance: The Distribution of Tax Revenue in the Ottoman Empire. *The Journal of Economic History* 65(3), 806–821.

Coşgel, M. and Miceli, T. (2009). Tax Collection in History. *Public Finance Review* 37, 399–420.

Çakır, B. (2006). Geleneksel Dönem (Tanzimat Öncesi) Osmanlı Bütçe Gelirleri. In M. Genç & E. Özvar (Eds.), *Osmanlı Maliyesi:Kurumlar ve Bütçeler I*, 167–196. Osmanlı Bankası Arşiv ve Araştırma Merkezi.

Çizakça, M. (1989). Tax-Farming and Resource Allocation in Past Islamic Societies. *Journal of King Abdulaziz University: Islamic Economics* 1, 59–80.

Çizakça, M. (1993). Tax-Farming and Financial Decentralization in the Ottoman Empire, 1520–1697. *The Journal of European Economic History* 22, 219–250.

Çizakça, M. (1996). *Comparative Evolution of Business Partnerships: The Islamic World and Europe, with Special Reference to the Ottoman Archives*. Brill.

Darling, L. (1996). *Revenue-Rising and Legitimacy: Tax Collection and Finance Administration in the Ottoman Empire, 1560–1660*. Leiden: Brill.

Drelichman, M. and Voth, H. (2011). Serial Defaults, Serial Profits: Returns to Sovereign Lending in Habsburg Spain, 1566–1600. *Explorations in Economic History* 48, 1–19.

Faroqhi, S. (2004). *The Ottoman Empire and the World Around It*. I. B. Tauris.

Genç, M. (2000). *Osmanlı İmparatorluğu'nda Devlet ve Ekonomi*. Ötüken.

Gintis, H. (2009). *Game Theory Evolving: A Problem-Centered Introduction to Modeling Strategic Interaction*. Princeton University Press.

Greene, M. (2000). *A Shared World, Christians and Muslims in the Early Modern Mediterranean*. Princeton University Press.

Greif, A. (2002). Economic History and Game Theory. In R. Aumann & S. Hart (Eds.), *Handbook of Game Theory with Economic Applications 3*, 1989–2024. North-Holland.

İnalcık, H. (2000). *Osmanlı İmparatorluğu'nun Sosyal ve Ekonomik Tarihi I*. Eren.

Johnson, N. D. (2006). Banking on the King: The Evolution of the Royal Revenue Farms in Old Regime France. *The Journal of Economic History*, 66(4), 963–991.

Johnson, N. D. and Koyama, M. (2014). Tax Farming and the Origins of State Capacity in England and France. *Explorations in Economic History* 51, 1–20.

Karaman, K. and Pamuk, Ş. (2010). Ottoman State Finance in European Perspective, 1500–1914. *The Journal of Economic History* 70, 593–629.

Kiel, M. (2009). Selanik. *İslam Ansiklopedisi* 36, 352–357.

Kiser, E. (1994). Markets and Hierarchies in Early Modern Tax Systems: A Principal-Agent Analysis. *Politics and Society*, 22, 284–315.

Kiser, E. and Schneider, J. (1994). Bureaucracy and Efficiency: An Analysis of Taxation in Early Modern Prussia. *American Sociological Review* 59, 187–204.

Kwass, M. (2000). *Privilege and the Politics of Taxation in Eighteenth-Century France*. Cambridge University Press.

Ma, D. and Rubin, J. (2019). The Paradox of Power: Principal-Agent Problems and Administrative Capacity in Imperial China (and Other Absolutist Regimes). *Journal of Comparative Economics* 47, 277–294.

North, D., Wallis, J. and Weingast, B. (2009). *Violence and Social Orders: A Conceptual Framework for Interpreting Recorded Human History*. Cambridge University Press.

North, D. and Weingast, B. (1989). Constitutions and Commitment: The Evolution of Institutions Governing Public Choice in Seventeenth-Century England. *The Journal of Economic History* 49, 803–832.

Özmucur, S. and Pamuk, Ş. (2002). Real Wages and Standards of Living in the Ottoman Empire, 1489–1914. *The Journal of Economic History* 62, 292–321.

Pamuk, Ş. (2000). The Ottoman Empire in the Eighteenth Century. *Itinerario* 24, 104–116.

Pamuk, Ş. (2009). Changes in Factor Markets in the Ottoman Empire, 1500–1800. *Continuity and Change* 24(1), 1–30.

Root, H. (1989). Tying the King's Hand: Credible Commitment and Royal Fiscal Policy during the Old Regime. *Rationality and Society* 1(2), 240–258.

Salzmann, A. (1993). An Ancien Regime Revisited: "Privatization" and Political Economy in the Eighteenth-Century Ottoman Empire. *Politics and Society* 21, 393–423.

Salzmann, A. (2004). *Tocqueville in the Ottoman Empire: Rival Paths to the Modern State*. Brill.

Vester, M. (2004). The Political Autonomy of a Tax Farm: The Nice-Piedmont Gabelle of the Dukes of Savoy, 1535–1580. *The Journal of Modern History* 76(4), 745–792.

White, E. (2004). From Privatized to Government-Administrated Tax Collection: Tax Farming in Eighteenth Century France. *The Economic History Review* 57, 636–663.

CHAPTER 9

Coordination and Conflict: A Game-Theoretic Assessment on the Fiscal Capacity Through Tax-Farming Contracts in the Early Modern Ottoman Empire

Bora Altay and Erkan Gürpınar

The development of fiscal capacity is a critical aspect of state-building in history, as it determines a state's ability to mobilize resources for public goods, warfare, and administrative governance. Among the various fiscal strategies adopted by the early modern states, tax farming has emerged as

B. Altay
Faculty of Political Sciences, Ankara Yıldırım Beyazıt University, Ankara, Türkiye
e-mail: boraaltay@aybu.edu.tr

E. Gürpınar (✉)
Faculty of Political Sciences, Social Sciences University of Ankara, Ankara, Türkiye
e-mail: erkan.gurpinar@asbu.edu.tr

B. Altay (ed.), *Revenue-Raising Institutions, State Organization and Economic Change in the Early Modern Ottoman Empire*, Palgrave Studies in Economic History,
https://doi.org/10.1007/978-3-031-96492-3_9

a widely implemented mechanism for ensuring revenue collection. In the Ottoman Empire, the tax-farming system (*Iltizam*) played a central role in financing the state's military, administrative, and infrastructural needs. By delegating tax collection to private individuals or groups in exchange for upfront payments or periodic revenue, the Ottoman state sought to overcome administrative inefficiencies and ensure a stable income flow. However, tax-farming contracts have also introduced significant coordination challenges, including conflicts between the state and its agents, the risk of opportunistic behavior, and difficulties in monitoring and enforcement. This chapter examines the dynamics of coordination and conflict inherent in Ottoman tax-farming contracts from a game-theoretic perspective. By analyzing the strategic interactions between the state (the principal) and tax farmers (the agents), we aim to elucidate how the Ottoman state addressed commitment problems and sought to resolve dilemmas in fiscal governance. The focus is on investigating the mechanisms that facilitate or impede the coordination of interests between the state and its agents, and how these dynamics influenced the broader trajectory of fiscal capacity development in the empire.

The Ottoman Empire's tax-farming methods underwent significant transformation from the early sixteenth century onward (Genç 2000; Pamuk 2004a). The transition from direct tax collection to tax farming reflected the state's efforts to adapt to increasing fiscal pressure, including military campaigns and administrative expansion (Salzmann 1993). Under the tax-farming institution, contracts were auctioned to the highest bidder, who subsequently collected taxes from a designated region or revenue source. This mechanism enabled the state to receive a stable revenue, mitigating the risks of tax collection by state officials and administrative inefficiencies. Over time, the malikane system—a lifetime tax-farming contract—emerged as a more stable alternative, providing tax farmers with long-term incentives for efficient revenue extraction.

Despite these advantages, tax farming is associated with numerous challenges. The state's dependence on private contractors creates opportunities for moral hazard, as tax farmers might exploit taxpayers or under-report revenue to maximize their profits. Moreover, there is an absence of robust mechanisms to enforce contracts and monitor compliance-exacerbated coordination problems. As the literature argues, these issues were not unique to the Ottoman Empire; they were shared by other early modern states that confronted similar dilemmas in balancing short-term fiscal needs with long-term institutional stability. In this context, this chapter aims to address the following research questions: How did the Ottoman state design tax-farming contracts to balance its fiscal objectives with the risks of opportunistic behavior? What role did institutional innovations play in mitigating conflicts and enhancing coordination between state and tax farmers? How does the Ottoman experience compare to other early modern states in terms of fiscal capacity development and institutional design? Utilizing game theory as an analytical framework, this study models the strategic interactions between the Ottoman state and tax farmers, elucidating the trade-offs inherent in tax-farming contracts. Through an examination of the interplay among incentives, monitoring mechanisms, and enforcement strategies, this study seeks to elucidate the conditions under which equilibrium is achieved.

This study contributes to several aspects of literature on fiscal capacity, institutional economics, and Ottoman history. First, it enhances the understanding of tax farming by applying a game-theory perspective to elucidate the dynamics of coordination (Greif 2002). While previous studies have documented the historical evolution of tax farming in the Ottoman Empire, this chapter provides a novel analytical framework to explain the persistence of coordination problems and solutions devised by the state (İslamoğlu and Keyder 1977; Salzmann 1993, 2004; Darling 1996; Çizakça 1996; Genç 2000; Abou-El-Haj 2000; Pamuk 2004a, 2004b; Karaman 2009; Balla and Johnson 2009; Karaman and Pamuk 2010). Second, the chapter bridges the economic history and institutional theory by examining the fiscal practices and state capacity from an analytical perspective. As a delegated revenue collection, tax farming represents a critical juncture in the evolution of fiscal institutions, wherein the state's ability to extract resources is contingent on its capacity to design effective contracts and enforce compliance. Hence, this study elucidates the institutional trade-offs faced by the Ottoman state and their implications for long-term fiscal stability. Third, the chapter presents a comparative perspective by contextualizing the Ottoman experience within the broader global patterns of fiscal capacity development. By comparing the Ottoman Empire's tax-farming mechanisms with alternative revenue extracting systems in Western Europe and China, this analysis elucidates the diverse institutional pathways adopted by early modern states and the factors that influenced their fiscal trajectories. This comparative examination contributes to the ongoing scholarly discourse on the origins of divergent developmental outcomes in state-building and economic performances (Kennedy 1988; Tilly 1990; Pomeranz 2000; Coşgel et al.

2009; Van Zanden 2009; Kuran 2011; Johnson and Koyama 2017; Rubin 2017; Ma and Rubin 2019). Through this analysis, this chapter aims to contribute to a more comprehensive understanding of the complex interrelationships between fiscal capacity, institutional design, and state-society relations in the early modern Ottoman Empire.

The remainder of this chapter is organized as follows. Section "Theoretical Framework" outlines the theoretical framework and introduces key game-theoretical concepts pertinent to the analysis of coordination and conflict in tax farming. Section "Tax-Farming Institutions in the Early Modern Ottoman Empire" provides a historical overview of tax farming in the Ottoman Empire, tracing its evolution from the classical to the early modern period and elucidating the institutional context in which it operated. Section "An Analytical Approach on Tax-Farming Contracts in the Ottoman Empire" examines the coordination problems inherent in tax-farming contracts, focusing on the strategic interaction between the state and tax farmers, and the mechanisms employed to mitigate conflicts in tax collection. Section "A Historical Perspective on How the State Capacity Was Affected by Contractual Relations" provides empirical evidence using tax-farming contracts in the city of Aleppo. Section "Implications of Findings" discusses the broader implications of the findings for fiscal capacity and institutional development, emphasizing the feedback loops between tax farming and state-building. Finally, section "Conclusion" summarizes the chapter by synthesizing key insights and proposing directions for future research.

Theoretical Framework

Understanding the fiscal capacity of early modern states necessitates a comprehensive examination of the institutional mechanisms that organize the relationship between the state and its agents. The Ottoman Empire's utilization of tax-farming contracts presents a particularly illuminating case for investigating tensions between coordination and conflict in resource governance. The delegation of revenue collection to private entities while addressing certain immediate fiscal challenges introduced complex coordination problems and raised questions regarding the design and sustainability of such arrangements. By integrating game-theoretic principles alongside Garrett Hardin's (1968) concept of the "tragedy of the commons," this perspective could elucidate the strategic interactions and institutional trade-offs inherent in Ottoman fiscal governance.

It is important to note that this analysis does not assert that Ottoman tax-farming contracts constitute a common good. However, the frequent transfer of these contracts during the process, their overutilization, and the subsequent reduction in welfare or benefits for subsequent tax farmers support the proposition that they align with the "tragedy of the commons" framework.

As in other early modern states, tax-farming contracts presented the challenge of aligning the state's fiscal objectives with the incentives of agents (Kiser 1999). As a principal, the Ottoman state sought to ensure stable revenue flows to support its short-term capital needs, including administrative and military organizations. Conversely, tax farmers, acting as agents, possessed incentives to maximize their individual profits, often at the expense of taxpayers and, consequently, the long-term fiscal structure of the state. This divergence of interests created a fundamental coordination problem characterized by opportunistic behavior, adverse selection, and enforcement difficulties (North and Weingast 1989; Root 1989; Greif 1989, 1993; North 1991, 1993; Williamson 1998).

Coordination problems arise when multiple actors fail to align their actions to achieve collective benefit. In the context of tax farming, this misalignment could result in exploitative practices, such as excessive taxation or underreporting of revenues, which undermined the state's fiscal aims. Furthermore, conflicts between the state and tax farmers were exacerbated by information asymmetry, as the state often lacked the capacity to monitor tax farmers' actions effectively. This imbalance hindered the enforcement of contracts and led to opportunistic behavior, resulting in inefficiencies, corruption, and diminished fiscal capacity (North and Weingast 1989).

Garrett Hardin's (1968) concept of the "tragedy of the commons" provides a robust analytical framework for examining the inherent tensions within the Ottoman tax-farming system. In Hardin's original formulation, individuals acting in their self-interest overexploit a shared resource, resulting in depletion and collective detriment. While Hardin applied this perspective to environmental resources, the concept is equally applicable to fiscal systems, wherein revenue can be conceptualized as a common resource that necessitates sustainable management and coordination.

Under the tax-farming system, the shared resource was the taxpayers' revenue-generating capacity. Tax farmers, motivated by the incentive to maximize their short-term profits, frequently extracted excessive taxes from their designated regions. This overextraction resulted in several detrimental effects; it diminished the productive capacity of local economies, incited taxpayer resistance, and reduced the state's ability to collect future revenue. Analogous to Hardin's tragedy of the commons, the absence of collective governance mechanisms led to the degradation of resources—in this case, the fiscal base of the Ottoman Empire.

The tragedy of the commons framework underscores the significance of institutional mechanisms in regulating resource utilization and preventing overexploitation. In the absence of such mechanisms, individual actors—whether herders in Hardin's original example or tax farmers in the Ottoman case—prioritize their short-term gains over the long-term sustainability of the resource. This perspective underscores the Ottoman state's critical role in designing institutions that align tax farmers' incentives with the broader fiscal objectives of the empire.

One of the main challenges in tax farming is designing contracts that align tax farmers' actions with the state fiscal objectives. For instance, contracts could include performance bonds or profit-sharing mechanisms to discourage opportunistic behavior and incentivize efficient revenue collection. The state often lacks complete information on the actions and revenues of tax farmers, making it difficult to detect fraud or inefficiency. This imbalance created opportunities for tax farmers to underreport revenues or engage in exploitative practices such as excessive taxation or rent-seeking. Many tax-farming contracts were periodically renewed, creating opportunities for reputation building between the state and tax farmers. In a repeated interaction framework, tax farmers might cooperate with the state to secure future contracts, thereby mitigating opportunistic behavior in the short term. Yet, both the state and tax farmers faced challenges in committing to their respective obligations. For the state, the temptation to renegotiate or revoke contracts in times of fiscal crisis created uncertainty for the tax farmers. Conversely, tax farmers often face incentives to exploit their positions before their contracts expire.

Game theory could provide a structured approach to modeling the strategic interactions between the Ottoman state and tax farmers. The principal-agent model is particularly useful in this context, as it captures the delegation of authority from the state to tax farmers and the challenges arising from information asymmetry and conflicting interests (Kiser 1994). This approach could also elucidate the broader dynamics of cooperation and conflict within the tax-farming institution. By identifying the conditions under which cooperative equilibria can emerge, this perspective provides insights into the institutional solutions adopted by the

Ottoman state to mitigate coordination problems and enhance its fiscal capacity.

The Ottoman state developed several institutional mechanisms to address the coordination problems and conflicts inherent in tax farming. Tax-farming contracts were often awarded through competitive auctions, enabling the state to maximize upfront payments and select contractors who demonstrated financial and managerial competence (Çizakça 1993). However, this system also incentivized tax farmers to extract excessive revenue to recover their initial investments. Secondly, requiring tax farmers to guarantors served as a financial safeguard against misconduct (Çizakça 1996, p. 149; İnalcık 2000, p. 105; Pamuk 2004b, p. 241). These guarantors provided the state with leverage to enforce compliance and deter opportunistic behavior. Thirdly, the state frequently relied on local elites or intermediaries to monitor tax farmers and to mediate disputes. These actors played a crucial role in bridging the information gap between the state and tax farmers, thus enhancing the effectiveness of the enforcement mechanisms. Finally, the transition from short-term tax farming to lifetime tax-farming contracts represented significant institutional innovation. By granting tax farmers lifetime rights to their contracts, the state created incentives for them to invest in the long-term productivity of their regions, aligning their interests with those of the state (Genç 2000; Pamuk 2004a). These institutional solutions highlight the adaptability of the Ottoman state in addressing the challenges posed by the tax-farming institutions. By balancing the need for immediate revenues with the risks of overextraction and conflict, the state sought to optimize its fiscal capacity while maintaining political and social stability.

The integration of game theory and the tragedy of the commons perspective provides a comprehensive framework for understanding the evolution of the Ottoman fiscal institutions. By addressing the coordination dilemmas and conflicts inherent in tax-farming contracts, the state sought to optimize resource extraction while mitigating the risks of overexploitation (Altay and Oğuz 2021). These strategies were instrumental in the development of fiscal capacity, as they enabled the state to sustain its administrative and military functions in the face of increasing challenges. Furthermore, the Ottoman experience offers broader insights into the relationship between institutional design and state-building. The efficacy of the Ottoman state in resolving coordination problems reflects the critical role of institutions in mediating the relationship between state and its agents under contractual relations. In this context, the tax-farming system provides a valuable case study for understanding the broader dynamics of fiscal governance and institutional development in the early modern states.

In sum, the theoretical framework presented herein shows the interplay between incentives, institutional design, and strategic behavior in the Ottoman tax-farming institution. By synthesizing game-theoretical analysis with insights from the tragedy of the commons, this chapter provides a nuanced understanding of the challenges and innovations in fiscal governance during the early modern period. This perspective not only enhances our comprehension of Ottoman fiscal capacity but also contributes to broader debates on state-building and institutional resilience.

Tax-Farming Institutions in the Early Modern Ottoman Empire

The tax-farming institution constituted a fundamental component of the Ottoman Empire's fiscal administration, playing a key role in maintaining its governance over its extensive territories. As the Ottoman state expanded across the three continents, the magnitude of its administrative and logistical challenges necessitated innovative approaches to revenue collection. Tax farming emerged as a pragmatic response to these challenges, facilitating the delegation of fiscal responsibilities to private entities while concurrently addressing the state's immediate liquidity requirements (Pamuk 2004b).

Over time, this institution underwent significant evolution, reflecting the shifting priorities and institutional capacities of the empire. From its inception in short-term tax-farming contracts to the subsequent implementation of long-term tax-farming contracts, the Ottoman tax-farming mechanisms exhibited remarkable adaptability until the early nineteenth century. Nevertheless, it was also characterized by inherent tensions and limitations that influenced the state's fiscal and political trajectories. A comprehensive understanding of the historical development, fiscal rationale, and institutional context of tax farming in the Ottoman Empire necessitated a nuanced examination of its mechanisms, advantages, and challenges.

The transition from direct tax collection to tax farming constituted one of the most significant transformations in the Ottoman Empire's fiscal history (Darling 1996). In its earliest phases, the empire relied extensively on the timar system, a mechanism that allocated land revenue to military officers and local elites in exchange for military services (Genç 2000, p. 102). The timar system functioned as both a fiscal and administrative framework, integrating local elites within the Ottoman hierarchy while ensuring a consistent flow of resources to support the state's military campaigns. This method proved efficacious during periods of expansion, as it enabled the state to consolidate control over newly conquered territories without necessitating costly and complex bureaucracy (İnalcık 2000, p. 105).

However, the limitations of the timar system became increasingly apparent as the Empire evolved and expanded. By the first decades of the fifteenth and early sixteenth centuries, the financial burden of maintaining a professional standing army coupled with the administrative complexities of governing remote provinces strained the system's capacity. To address these challenges, the state required a more adaptable and efficient means of collecting revenue. The implementation of the tax-farming institution marked a significant development in this regard, as it enabled the state to delegate tax collection to private contractors, while securing immediate monetary inflows for the treasury (Darling 1996, pp. 119–120).

Under the tax-farming institution, tax collection rights were auctioned to the highest bidder, who remitted a highest annual payment to the state in exchange for the right to collect taxes from a specific region or revenue source within a predetermined period. This arrangement provided the state with stable liquidity and directly reduced the administrative burden of managing tax collection. However, it also engendered new challenges, as the short-term nature of tax-farming contracts incentivized tax farmers to maximize their profits at the expense of local populations.

The fiscal and administrative pressures of the late seventeenth century, including prolonged military conflicts and internal unrest, necessitated further innovation within the institutional environment. The introduction of lifetime contracts represented a significant departure from the short-term logic of tax-farming contracts. These long-term or lifetime contracts aimed to stabilize revenue streams and align the interests of tax farmers with those of the state. Unlike tax-farming contracts, lifetime contracts required tax farmers to make both an initial lump-sum payment (*muaccele*) and regular annual installments, thereby incentivizing them to invest in the long-term productivity of their regions (Genç 2000, p. 108).

The Ottoman tax-farming institution was predicated on a clear fiscal rationale that aimed to balance the state's immediate revenue requirements with administrative constraints. Concurrently, the system's efficacy was contingent upon navigating a complex network of institutional challenges, including issues of monitoring, enforcement, and commitment problem. Pragmatic fiscal considerations precipitated the implementation of tax farming in the Ottoman Empire. The tax-farming system conferred several advantages to the state. First, upfront payments made by tax farmers provided the treasury with immediate access to funds, which was crucial for financing military campaigns, administrative expenditures, and other state functions. This liquidity was particularly significant during periods of fiscal strain such as prolonged wars or economic downturns. Second, by delegating tax collection to private contractors, the state mitigated the logistical and bureaucratic challenges in managing the vast empire. This delegation allowed the state to allocate its resources to core governance functions such as maintaining internal security and defending its borders. Third, tax farming transferred the risks associated with revenue collection, such as crop failures, market fluctuations, or local resistance, to private actors (Darling 1996, p. 119; Coşgel and Miceli 2005, 2009). This arrangement insulated the state from financial volatility and ensured more predictable revenue flow.

Tax-farming and lifetime contracts presented significant economic and social opportunities for tax farmers. First, the successful administration of tax-farmed regions enabled contractors to generate substantial profits, often significantly exceeding their initial investments. This profit potential attracted a diverse range of participants including affluent merchants, urban elites, and religious endowments (waqfs). Second, the wealth and influence accumulated through tax farming facilitated the social mobility of many agents (*Mültezims*). Some utilized their positions to secure political appointments or establish themselves as local power brokers and further intertwined fiscal and political dynamics. Third, under lifetime contracts, the perpetual nature of agreements provided tax farmers with a degree of security, encouraging them to invest in their regions and establish enduring networks of influence.

Despite its advantages, the tax-farming institution was fraught with challenges that shaped its implementation and outcome. First, the state's capacity to monitor tax farmers' activities was constrained by its administrative capability (Altay and Oğuz 2021). This lack of oversight created opportunities for corruption, underreporting, and overextraction, thereby undermining the efficiency and equity of the system. Second, ensuring compliance with tax-farming contracts required robust enforcement mechanisms, which were often lacking. Disputes between the state and tax farmers, or between tax farmers and local populations, frequently led to conflicts that strained the system's stability. Third, the short-term nature of tax-farming contracts created strong incentives for tax farmers to prioritize immediate profits over long-term sustainability. While lifetime contracts addressed some of these issues, they introduced new risks such as the concentration of fiscal power in the hands of a few elites. Finally, the extractive practices of tax farmers often had significant social and economic ramifications. Excessive taxation reduced agricultural productivity, disrupted local markets, and provoked resistance in local populations. These dynamics not only undermined the legitimacy of the Ottoman administration, but also hindered the empire's capacity to maintain effective governance.

Therefore, examining the historical background of Ottoman tax farming from a game-theoretical perspective is essential to comprehending the strategic interactions between the state and tax farmers. Game theory provides a framework for analyzing how each actor's decisions are influenced by incentives, constraints, and the behavior of others within the institutional environment. For instance, the Ottoman state's delegation of tax collection to agents can be conceptualized as a principal-agent problem, wherein the state (the principal) relies on tax farmers (agents) to maximize revenue while minimizing the risk of corruption and overextraction. Tax farmers, in turn, face a trade-off between maximizing short-term profits and maintaining long-term sustainability, particularly under lifetime contracts. By applying game theory, scholars can elucidate the underlying commitment problems, incentive structures, and enforcement challenges that have shaped the evolution and outcomes of Ottoman fiscal institutions. This analytical approach not only enhances our understanding of the Ottoman tax-farming system but also offers broader insights into the dynamics of delegated governance and institutional design in premodern states.

An Analytical Approach on Tax-Farming Contracts in the Ottoman Empire

Ottoman tax-farming contracts, while innovative and adaptable, inherently generated coordination challenges between the state and tax farmers. These issues arose primarily from the conflicting incentives, information asymmetries, and difficulties in monitoring that characterized the relationship. Coordination challenges were most pronounced in the strategic interactions between the state and tax farmers, the implementation of contractual innovations to mitigate conflicts, and the role of institutions in resolving dilemmas that emerged in the fiscal system. Game theory provides a valuable analytical framework for examining these dynamics and elucidating how strategic decisions by various actors influence the efficiency and stability of the tax-farming system.

Garrett Hardin (1968)'s *Tragedy of the Commons* provides a compelling theoretical framework for analyzing coordination problems in Ottoman tax farming. Hardin's model elucidates a scenario in which individual actors, motivated by rational self-interest, overexploit shared resources, resulting in collective detriment. In the context of Ottoman tax farming, the commons can be conceptualized as the productive capacity of the tax base (e.g., peasants, land, customs, or commercial activity). Tax farmers, analogous to Hardin's herdsmen, operate under incentives that encourage the maximization of short-term gains, potentially at the expense of long-term sustainability.

As mentioned above, the Ottoman state allocated financial resources to tax farmers and granted them authority to collect revenue within a defined jurisdiction. However, while the state sought stable and sustainable revenue streams, tax farmers frequently regarded the tax base as a finite resource for exploitation during the contract period. Under short-term contracts, individual tax farmers lacked incentives to preserve the productivity of the commons (the tax base) because they did not internalize the costs of their exploitation. These dynamic parallels Hardin's tragedy, in which rational actors degrade their shared resources because of their inability to coordinate.

From a game theoretic perspective, tax farmers faced the following options: (1) sustainable tax, thereby investment in the local economy or (2) maximizing extraction for immediate (or short term) profits. Because tax farmers competed in auctions to secure their contracts—often paying high upfront sums—their focus shifted to recovering their initial costs. This created a cycle of exploitation, as each farmer anticipated that others would similarly deplete resources, thus encouraging pre-emptive over-taxation. The state was confronted with a coordination dilemma. While auctioning contracts to the highest bidder provided immediate revenue, it also exacerbated the moral hazard and tragedy of the commons. Short-term fiscal pressures compelled the state to prioritize immediate income over long-term economic stability, further entrenching the cycle of overextraction.

The dilemma here is that there may be many reasons to prefer a Pareto-inefficient outcome over a Pareto-efficient outcome; all that is precluded is a preference for a particular outcome when some other feasible outcome is Pareto superior. The reason why uncoordinated activities of individuals pursuing their own ends often produce outcomes that all would seek to avoid is that each person's actions affect the well-being of others, and these effects are often not included in whatever optimizing process or rule of thumb results in decisions made by self-interested actors. What rules govern interactions among people that would simultaneously facilitate the pursuit of their own ends, while inducing each to take adequate account of the effects of their actions on others? Any solution to coordination problems will be substantially decentralized, and none that seeks to simply override individual intentions is either workable or desirable. Where a person's actions unavoidably affect the well-being of others, how can these effects be made sufficiently salient to influence the actor's behavior in appropriate ways? The changing economic environment, developments in productive processes, and increasing number of players have caused the challenge of designing institutions that work well: ***the theory of mechanism design*** and ***optimal contract theory***.

The State and agent made contractual arrangements under certain conditions. The state preferred to give contracts to local agents instead of collecting taxes directly. That is the former method was more beneficial than the latter (or at least as beneficial as the latter) in terms of tax revenues. Several reasons, stemming mainly from asymmetric information, could be behind this policy choice. Whatever the reason, relying on local authorities meant higher tax revenues for the state. Let us denote the tax revenue of the state under tax farming as t, and tax revenues when employing state officials (that is the direct method) as t_f. Then, for the state, the fallback position (or next best alternative of employing state officials) was not higher than the tax-farming contract, i.e., $t > t_f > 0$. The incentives for the agents, under the tax-farming institution, also changed with the new rules of the game. Formerly, agents in the traditional timar institution were mostly military-based individuals, and they could obtain contracts regarding their achievements during campaigns. The military agents had a lower chance of choosing their contracts with calculating costs and benefits of the land they willing to obtain. The changing structure of agents enabled them to choose their contracts in order to maximize their gains from contractual arrangements. If an agent offered the highest price to take a contract, the contractual relationships would be established.

It was also the case that for agents taking the contract (offered by the central authority) was preferred to not taking it. This means that, for the agents, profits obtained from the tax-farming relation was higher than their fallback option (or next best alternative of not taking a contract). If a local agent does not take a contract, he obtains revenues mainly from trade or agricultural production. Yet, what they get from the tax-farming contract was higher. Tax-farming contracts did not only increase economic revenues but also political power for local agents. That is, tax-farming contracts enabled local agents to capture gains from the state offices they obtained. For instance, an agent, who was able to take a state office through a contract, could gain substantial revenues in addition to economic privileges of tax-farming contracts. Both archival documents and historical studies showed that agents also had strong incentives to obtain tax-farming contracts from the State. If we denote the profit obtained by an agent when the tax-farming contract is taken as p, and his fallback option as p_f, we have $p > p_f > 0$.

However, in this relation, the State usually did not honor contract duration, which was usually between one and twelve years. In these cases, the strategies of the state and agents failed to secure contracts and achieve cooperation among the state and local agents. In retrospect, the failure of achieving cooperation between the contracting parties could be related to do the short sightedness of both parties in the relation. The state was concerned, as we pointed out above, with short-term revenue raising due to urgent needs of the central budget; therefore, in response, local agents paid more attention to short run profit maximization rather than to investment in land, which, indeed, had a potential to increase revenues for both in the long run. The institutional structure was such that, short-term contracts were one of the main problems of profit-seeking activities and investment incentives, uncertainty was another major problem that emerged. The strategic interaction between the state and local agents, which was carried out non-cooperatively (i.e., they decide separately without any binding agreement) led to an outcome none would prefer. To put it differently, there was an economic incentive for both parties to engage in tax farming. However, the institutional structure was such that it led to a Nash equilibrium which is not Pareto efficient, i.e., prisoner's dilemma (Figs. 9.1 and 9.2).

Strategies of the state and agents would determine the characteristic of the equilibrium that affected the economic performance of the Ottoman Empire. We argue that while one set of strategies favored long-run economic development (which is the Pareto-efficient outcome), the institutional structure led parties to lock into the alternative set of strategies (Nash equilibrium) focusing on only the short-run benefits of the relation. Archival evidence points to two critical issues under the rules of the game. The State had a coercive power on all over the empire, that is it had the power to not to honor contracts; and agents, particularly unemployed agents, could always make a new offer for a contract even this contract was arranged very recently.

To study how institutional mechanisms was working and what mechanisms emerged as the solution of problems, alternative strategies of the parties and possible equilibrium/equilibria of the interaction should be

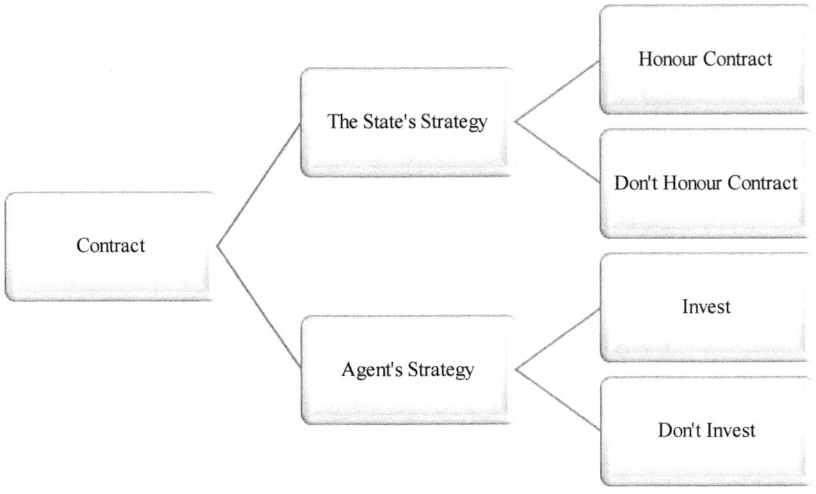

Fig. 9.1 The strategies of the state and agents in a contract

		State	
		honour	don't honour
Agent	invest	p_e, t_e	0, t_d
	don't invest	p_d, 0	p, t

Fig. 9.2 Payoffs under a tax-farming contract

analyzed in detail. Recall that we have already defined the benefits (that is payoffs) of tax-farming contract to the state and agents as t and p, respectively. Assume that the state and an agent interact for a tax-farming contract. Assume further that the state has two strategies regarding the terms of the contract: {honor, don't honor}. Similarly, the agent has two strategies regarding the land under the terms (hence duration) of the contract: {invest, don't invest}. They each knew that if the agent invests on the land, and if the state honors the contract, they could each be better off. However, at the same time, there were strong incentives to act differently for both. Assume that the state and an agent act simultaneously and they only care about their own material payoffs (tax revenue and profits). That is, we describe a typical tax-farming contract between the state and an agent in the Ottoman Empire.

For simplicity, assume that unilateral cooperation yields zero benefit. This is the case when either the state plays honor, or the agent plays invest. For example, when the state does not honor the contract, but the agent invests in land, he incurs loses in his investment. This situation, in fact, has a dual effect on the agent. First, the agent would direct financial resources to receive a contract in auctions. The more intense the competition, the higher the price for the contract. The cost of getting a contract means that, indeed, auctions absorb substantial share of financial resources of agents. Therefore, once the State choose not to honor the contract, the agent faces the problem to losing his invested financial resources. Secondly, when the state does not honor the contract, the agent may also lose his political powers. Thus, the agent may lose his power to participate in future auctions. On the other hand, if the state honors the contract but the agent chooses not to invest in the land, there will be a loss of tax revenues due to unproductive use of the land by the agent. Similar to the former situation, opportunistic behavior of agents has two major effects on the revenues of the state. First, the agents could use their ability to crop higher shares from tax revenues of the state. Second, the agents had also the ability to exploit financial resources through economic activities that provide short-term gains, which lead to long-term unproductivity.

The choice of the agents, in this sense, entails losses in the value of the contracts. Consequently, the state ends up receiving lower offers for these financial resources. In sum, unilateral cooperation is not preferable as long as each contracting party had the ability to obtain higher returns from opportunistic behavior as described above. The historical evidence of the short-term nature of the contracts showed that the State was short sighted, and this directed the agents toward opportunistic behavior, in which short-term gains were preferable. The tax-farming relation is a prisoner's dilemma under the following conditions: $p > 0$, $t > 0$, $p_d > p_e$, $t_d > t_e$.

Let us define $\alpha = t_d - t_e$ and $\mu = p_d - p_e$ where the last two parameters denote the extra benefits of unilateral defection (i.e., free-riding) for the state and the agent, respectively. The most important reason for such an outcome is that the State could always seize the contract in order to increase its revenues by reallocating it with a new auction toward agents, i.e., *don't honor* is a strictly dominant strategy for the State. By doing so, the state was able to maximize (short run) tax revenues by continuously transferring tax-farming rights to other agents in the interaction. Additional tax revenues gained from this strategy is denoted by α. Similarly, for the agent, using the land with a short-term view focusing on rent-seeking activities raises his profits, since the alternative could lead to profit loss due to arbitrary termination of the contractual relation, i.e., *don't invest* is a strictly dominant strategy for the agent. Denote extra benefits from this strategy by μ.

These extra benefits emerge mainly from the fact that the State was not able to allocate enough resources to efficiently monitor the agents' activity. Being aware of the limited monitoring capabilities of the state, agents directed their activities to rent-seeking that provided higher short-term gains. The recent literature, in parallel with our model, argues that the deterioration of monitoring mechanism of the state occurred at the same time with the institutional change which led to the tax-farming contract. An important aspect of this development is related to the fact that agents who receive these contracts acquired political power, which in turn increased the costs of monitoring their activities by the state. In this relation, however, mutual cooperation was the Pareto-efficient outcome (even though not the Nash equilibrium), i.e., $t_e > t$ and $p_e > p$. The agent would have the necessary incentives to invest in the land and increase not only his profits but also the future tax revenues collected by the state, knowing that the tax-farming contract would be honored. In this case, the state would increase her tax revenues since the agent's investment on the land would increase productivity and generate higher revenues in the long run.

The payoff for strong cooperation is feasible and implementable by the "honoring contract and invest" rule, but more complex agreements can implement any point within the set *abcd* in Fig 9.3. Of course, the State

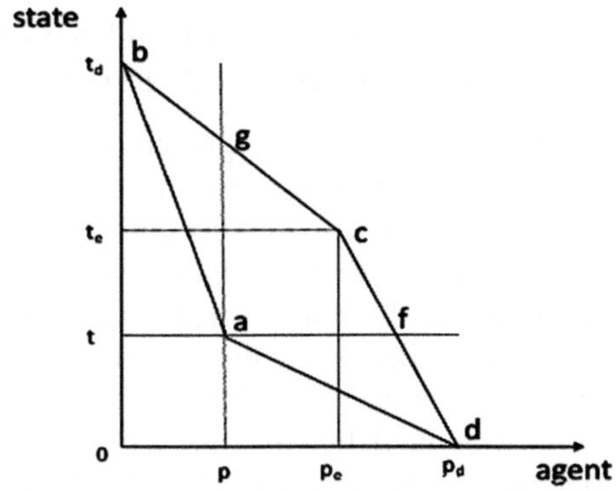

Fig. 9.3 Coordination and conflict: the state capacity in analytical form

would reject any offer along *fd*. Pareto-efficient agreements are all the points along *fcg*. The agent, then, might reject the disadvantageous offers along *bg* by the state. Bowles (2004, p. 30) provides further discussion on the implications of the figure in a Prisoner's Dilemma Game.

If the state and agent cannot agree on a division, it may be that no agreement to restrict choices of players is possible. But a third party, the courts, might impose a punishment on both players and then let them bargain to some more refined agreement if they are able to do so. Or the players come to adhere to a norm inducing each independently to restrict their opportunistic strategies. The norm would imply a new payoff matrix in which the concern about collective damage on gains. It is just this type of indeterminacy that economic and other institutions address, answering such questions as who is positioned to make a take-it-or-leave-it offer, what other actions are available to the relevant parties, what information asymmetries or lack of verifiability bear on the problem (and, as a result, what agreements are enforceable by third parties), and what norms may affect the outcome of the conflict. Information sharing among players discourages cheating, while legal regulations supplement local social-network-based enforcement (Ostrom 1990). We need to explore the analytics of how taxes, asymmetric power relations among actors, social norms, and other aspects of social interactions affect outcomes.

A Historical Perspective on How the State Capacity Was Affected by Contractual Relations

As demonstrated in the preceding section, the rules of the game theoretically indicate that tax-farming contracts in the Ottoman Empire were in a Pareto-inefficient equilibrium. Specifically, it is demonstrated that the state's fiscal capacity provides less tax revenue than anticipated, owing to the limits of the state capacity. The fundamental assumption herein is that taxes are collected in inefficient or Pareto inferior equilibrium resulting from this limited capacity of the state, e.g., the lack of "take-it-or-leave-it" power held by the state. The extent to which these equilibria were determined according to the rules of the game necessitates an examination through historical primary sources. This study provides empirical evidence using tax-farming contracts in the city of Aleppo in the late sixteenth century, during the Ottoman Empire.

Tax-farming contracts have several limitations. These primary sources are dispersed throughout the Ottoman archives. Consequently, identifying consecutive contracts is a challenging task. However, some studies focus on specific contracts from reliable secondary sources. One of the most significant of these is the study by Murat Çizakça (1993), which examined the competitive structure of contracts. The dataset utilized in this study includes consecutive tax-farming contracts. However, because this study focuses on the competitive structure of contracts, it provides the prices that emerge in auctions and the annual payments expected to be paid by agents in nominal terms. In this study, two examples of contracts pertaining to the city of Aleppo are utilized. The first example is the tax-farming contract offered for olive oil and soap. The second comprises tax-farming contracts based on flour production. To elucidate the state and fiscal capacity more clearly and comprehend the resulting equilibria more precisely, we present the monetary values of these contracts in real terms. To deflate the nominal values, this analysis refers to the Istanbul consumer price index, which is widely used in the literature (Pamuk 2004c).

Table 9.1 presents the data for two contracts transferred to tax farmers by auction in Aleppo, the Ottoman Empire, in the late sixteenth century. An examination of the table reveals discrepancies between the intended and actual durations for both samples. These discrepancies theoretically indicate commitment problems. However, these issues may arise for several reasons. First, tax farmers who submitted higher bids in auctions may have agreed to excessive payment terms and failed to assess the sustainability of the contract accurately. This phenomenon is observed in the first two Olive Oil and Soap contracts. The first contract shows that a tax farmer acquired tax collection rights for this financial resource in exchange for approximately 54 thousand akçe per annum. As it is seen that after two years when a farmer with a different tax submitted a higher bid, the state exercised its authority to transfer this contract to a new tax farmer. The annual payment for this new contract increases to approximately 98 thousand akçe. It is logical and pragmatic for the state that received a higher bid to transfer this contract to the new tax farmer. One of the most significant issues to consider is the assumption that a state utilizes its absolute power. Such a change in the contract holder may be attributed to the inability of the previous tax farmer to fulfill contractual obligations.

The termination of the contract with an annual payment of 98 thousand akçe after two years and its subsequent reallocation through auction in 1587 indicates a significant deviation from the established pattern. In the new contract of 1587, the annual tax payment decreased to 28 thousand akçe. Despite the four-year duration of this contract, it was transferred to a different tax farmer through an auction one year

Table 9.1 Tax-farming contracts in Aleppo (in akçe, 1469 prices)

Contract	*Year*	*Intended duration*	*Actual duration*	*Auction price*	*Annual payments*
Olive oil and soap	1581	4	2	217.890	54.472
	1583	4	2	392.180	98.045
	1587	4	1	113.314	28.329
	1588	4	1	91.685	22.921
	1589	4	2	132.039	33.010
	1591	4	1	130.816	32.704
	1592	4	2	142.208	35.552
Flour market	1583	3	1	202.037	67.346
	1584	4	2	172.768	43.192
	1585	4	1	206.356	51.589
	1586	5	3	183.159	36.632
	1589	4	2	162.265	40.566
	1591	4	1	151.480	37.870
	1592	3	2	105.195	35.065

Source Çizakça (1993: 236–250)

later. The annual payment of the contract in 1588 further decreased to approximately 22 thousand akçe. These reductions in annual payments are primarily attributable to the effects of external shocks rather than a commitment problem. Tax-farming contracts based on agricultural production are more susceptible to environmental and climatic factors than are customs contracts. During this period, a drought or alternative climatic event that likely occurred in the city of Aleppo in the Ottoman Empire adversely affected the production capacity. Consequently, the decrease in production led to a reduction in annual income, prompting tax farmers pursuing profit maximization to secure contracts by offering lower bids.

Similar trends are also observed in the flour market contracts of the city of Aleppo during the Ottoman Empire. Contracts with decreases in annual payments and values, particularly due to external factors, such as climatic shocks, frequently undergo modifications. While increasing bids in annual payments in certain periods compels the state to transfer contracts to new tax farmers, the prices and tax revenues of contracts occasionally decrease because of the effects of external shocks. The other variables warrant consideration. The possibility that the previous tax farmer may overexploit agricultural land to maximize short-term profits may also result in a decrease in tax revenues in the subsequent auction period. Under the assumption that tax farmers, who are expected to conduct the most accurate profit-loss analyses on a tax-farming contract and operate as private entrepreneurs, provide the most accurate price, the opportunistic behavior of previous tax farmers based on overexploitation should not be disregarded in price decreases. To monitor these factors and mitigate overexploitation, state capacity should be substantial. It is crucial not only to develop and implement monitoring mechanisms effectively but also to ensure that legal sanctions are enforceable.

In tax-farming contracts, a guarantor was predominantly required by tax farmers. These guarantors were comprised of Muslims and non-Muslims with a specified level of wealth. If a tax farmer encountered difficulties in making annual payments or fails to pay, these payments were collected from guarantors. Furthermore, when payment issues or opportunistic behaviors of tax farmers were identified, the state imposed legal penalties on these entities. These penalties were documented under the "Nezir Hücceti" in the Ottoman archives (Anastasopoulos 2011). However, it was challenging to ascertain the extent to which monetary penalties are enforced effectively. In other words, while there was no conclusive evidence regarding the enforceability of legal penalties, it was not possible to assert that tax farmers adhered to their contracts without any issues. Considering that treasury revenues stagnated, particularly in the sixteenth century, it could be postulated that the efficacy of such legal sanctions was limited. Nevertheless, the increasing revenues of the central treasury in the seventeenth century, attributed to the effect of long-term contracts, might be sufficient to suggest that legal sanctions had a positive impact. However, it was not feasible to generalize these findings to all types of contracts.

Therefore, alternative methodologies should be employed to assess the impact of these contracts on Ottoman central treasury revenue. One such approach is to evaluate the equilibria that emerge based on the theoretical framework established through game theory by utilizing primary sources. The contracts examined in this study provide significant data. First, the auction prices and duration of the contracts are known. Second, it is possible to calculate annual payments using these data and to determine the long-term revenues generated by the treasury. The fundamental questions can be formulated as follows: If the tax farmer who secured the initial contract had maintained the contract under the original conditions for an extended period during the auctions, what would have been the treasury's revenue? Conversely, what was the state's revenues from auctions for the Central Treasury? The primary hypothesis posits that, according to theoretical approaches, if a contract had been held by a tax farmer for an extended period without commitment issues arising, the state's revenues would have been higher. Conversely, if the state had continuously transferred the contract to different tax farmers using its authority, revenue would have decreased. In other words, according to the first assumption, the equilibrium that emerges will be at point a, whereas according to the second assumption, equilibrium will occur at point c. An institutional structure in which equilibrium a provides a greater payoff than equilibrium c results in missed opportunities for increased income.

A challenge that arises in this approach is that, if income decreases due to external factors, such as climatic conditions, maintaining the same tax farmer for an extended period may still result in reduced revenue. Nevertheless, this issue may facilitate the recovery of the difference from the guarantor, as it will diminish the state's monitoring costs owing to the contract being held by a single farmer. Engaging in a scenario with fewer participants rather than multiple parties will minimize coordination problems and revenue loss. Furthermore, tax farmers who will retain the contract for an extended duration will be incentivized to invest while considering these external factors. This incentive is crucial for minimizing risks that may arise in subsequent periods. An agent assured that their contract will not be terminated due to a lower tax payment will be motivated to manage their risks accordingly and increase their capital for future period payments. In essence, a single tax farmer holding a long-term contract in an institutional environment with minimal commitment problems creates greater incentives to minimize tax revenue losses.

Table 9.2 empirically demonstrates the revenue loss attributable to insufficient state capacity. The state, employing auctions to maximize revenue, consistently allocates relevant contracts to various tax farmers. During these transition periods, annual payments fluctuated in accordance with external factors and participants' strategies. The revenues generated as a result of this differentiation correspond to point a, which represents the equilibrium arising from the commitment problem (See Fig. 9.3). However, if the contracts remained with the initial tax farmer and the interaction continued uninterrupted, the anticipated revenue would have been higher, shifting the equilibrium toward point c. While it cannot be definitively asserted that the equilibrium coincides precisely with point a, the data presented in the table suggest proximity to point *a*, accounting for external shocks and the evolving institutional environment. The final column of Table 9.2 illustrates the discrepancies between the long-term contract secured through the initial auction and the subsequent auction-derived contracts. This disparity reflects the revenue differential between equilibria *a* and *c* (c–a), as depicted in Fig. 9.3, which is attributable to relatively limited state capacity. These findings suggest that rather than distributing tax-farming contracts through auctions for short-term periods, a contract awarded via auction should remain with a single tax farmer. Although this hypothesis is theoretically supported by empirical evidence, it does not alter the fact that it represents the most effective method available to the state, given the prevailing conditions and influence of extensive geography. The state's efforts and necessity to maintain equilibrium in its relations with local powers may have necessitated periodic redistribution of contracts among various groups. In light of this consideration, results that integrate theoretical and historical analyses should be interpreted with caution.

Table 9.2 Possible tax-farming contract revenues under different cases (in akçe, 1469 prices)

Contract	c *(keeping contract for All periods)*	a *(frequent auctions)*	c–a *(loss of revenue under lower state capacity)*
Olive oil and soap	871,560	526,112	345,447
Flour market	875,496	504,347	371,149
Both contracts	1,747,055	1,030,459	716,596

Implications of Findings

The findings from the analysis of Ottoman tax-farming contracts and their associated coordination challenges offer significant implications for understanding the interplay between the state and fiscal capacity in historical contexts. These findings underscore how institutional structures and strategic interactions shape fiscal performance, and contribute to broader debates on state formation, resource management, and economic development. In this context, this study demonstrates that the Ottoman state's reliance on short-term tax-farming contracts driven by immediate revenue requirements frequently resulted in suboptimal fiscal outcomes. The recurrent reallocation of contracts and absence of commitment to long-term agreements introduced inefficiencies that impeded sustainable revenue generation. This phenomenon highlights a fundamental trade-off faced by premodern states: the necessity to balance short-term revenue extraction with the long-term stability and productivity of tax bases. As earlier studies argue that less corruption and commitment problem surrounded the institutional environment between the mid-sixteenth and mid-seventeenth centuries (Darling 1996, p. 119; Altay and Oğuz 2021, p. 80). From the late seventeenth centuries onward, the problems in tax-farming contracts increases due to the external and internal factors. The implication for state capacity is twofold: states with more robust commitment mechanisms could generate more stable revenues, as long-term contracts incentivize tax farmers to invest in the productivity of their tax bases rather than to overexploit them (Root 1989; North and Weingast 1989). These findings underscore the importance of institutional structures that align tax farmers' incentives with a state's long-term fiscal objectives (Kiser 1999). Mechanisms such as enforceable guarantees, credible legal sanctions, and consistent monitoring can mitigate opportunistic behaviors and ensure greater revenue stability (North 1991).

This study situates Ottoman tax-farming contracts within the framework of game theory, particularly the Tragedy of the Commons and Prisoner's dilemma. These models elucidate how coordination failures and incentives between the state and tax farmers lead to suboptimal Nash equilibrium, where both parties prioritize short-term benefits over Pareto-efficient outcomes. The parallels between historical tax farming and modern public–private partnerships (PPPs) underscore the enduring relevance of designing contracts that mitigate coordination problems. The Ottoman experience suggests that decentralized revenue collection systems require robust institutional arrangements to manage information asymmetries and ensure accountability (Balla and Johnson 2009). Mechanism design theory has emerged as a key tool to address the challenge of aligning individual incentives with collective welfare. This approach can guide policymakers in structuring contracts that internalize externalities and promote cooperative behavior.

This study also identifies the impact of external shocks, such as climatic events, on the revenue potential of tax-farming contracts. These shocks compounded commitment problems by making long-term revenue forecasts uncertain and increasing the state's reliance on short-term solutions. A significant contribution of this analysis is its emphasis on the importance of state capacity in managing external risk. By fostering institutions that can absorb shocks through mechanisms such as flexible contracts, revenue insurance schemes, and diversification of revenue streams, states can stabilize their fiscal systems and enhance their resilience.

The findings challenge the simplistic narratives of the Ottoman decline by offering a nuanced perspective of its fiscal challenges. The inefficiencies in tax-farming contracts were not merely symptomatic of broader administrative decay but rather reflective of deliberate trade-offs in a resource-constrained and geographically expansive empire. This perspective aligns with revisionist approaches that view the Ottoman Empire's fiscal policies as adaptive rather than inherently flawed. By situating these policies within the broader context of state-building and revenue optimization, this study contributes to ongoing scholarly debates on the evolution of fiscal institutions in premodern states (Monson and Schneidel 2015; Johnson and Koyama 2017).

Comparative insights derived from game theoretic models provide a valuable framework for analyzing fiscal systems across diverse historical contexts. The Ottoman experience offers insights into understanding how early modern states in Europe and Asia managed similar challenges in resource mobilization and coordination. The findings encourage a comparative analysis of Ottoman fiscal policies with those of other empires, such as the Ming and Qing dynasties in China and early modern European states (Ma and Rubin 2019). These comparisons could elucidate how various institutional designs influence fiscal capacity and economic development. By analyzing the complex dynamics of Ottoman tax farming, this study enhances our understanding of the historical interrelationships between state capacity, fiscal policy, and institutional design. Its contributions to scholarly literature extend beyond the Ottoman context, providing valuable insights for the examination of fiscal systems in both historical and contemporary settings.

Conclusion

This chapter examines the complex interplay between state capacity, institutional design, and the resolution of commitment problems in fiscal systems, utilizing the tax-farming arrangements of the Ottoman Empire as a case study. Through an analysis of the challenges presented by short-term contracts, opportunistic behaviors, and external shocks, the discussion demonstrates the crucial role of credible commitments and institutional flexibility in ensuring long-term fiscal and economic stability. The Ottoman state's inability to effectively align tax farmers' incentives with broader economic objectives underscores a recurring theme in premodern governance: the tension between immediate revenue requirements and sustainable resource management.

The analysis further emphasizes the broader implications of institutional structures on state-society relations. Inadequate enforcement mechanisms, coupled with limited avenues for collaboration between central authorities and local agents, resulted in erosion of trust and inefficiencies in resource allocation. These issues underscore the necessity of institutional mechanisms that reduce transaction costs, ensure equitable enforcement, and balance the risks and rewards faced by economic actors. In addition to contributing to the historical understanding, the discussion has provided insights into broader theoretical frameworks, particularly in game theory. The recurring dilemmas of cooperation, resource overexploitation, and suboptimal equilibria reflect the enduring challenges that transcend historical contexts. By situating these issues within a structured analytical framework, this chapter offers valuable lessons for understanding the interplay between economic incentives and institutional constraints, in both historical and contemporary settings.

Future research should investigate the interplay between state capacity, institutional design, and commitment problems in diverse historical and geographic contexts. Comparative studies between the Ottoman tax-farming system and other revenue collection methods, such as European tax systems or Chinese fiscal institutions, could provide deeper insights into how different states navigated similar challenges. Additionally, examining the role of external factors, such as environmental shocks or geopolitical pressures, in shaping fiscal strategies would enhance our understanding of how institutions adapt to uncertainty. Game-theoretic models can be expanded to include multi-period and multi-actor frameworks to better capture the long-term dynamics of cooperation and resource sustainability. Furthermore, archival studies that focus on specific tax-farming contracts and local-level interactions can elucidate how regional variations influence the effectiveness of fiscal policies.

References

Abou-El-Haj, R. A. (2000). *Modern Devletin Doğası: 16. Yüzyıldan 18. Yüzyıla Osmanlı İmparatorluğu* (translated by Oktay Özel and Canay Şahin). İmge Kitabevi.

Altay, B. and Oğuz, F. (2021). *Rules, Contracts and Law Enforcement in the Ottoman Empire: The Case of Tax-Farming Contracts*. Palgrave Macmillan.

Anastasopoulos, A. (2011). Political Participation, Public Order, and Monetary Pledges (Nezir) in Ottoman Crete. In E. Gara, M. E. Kabadayı & C. K. Neumann (Eds.), *Popular Protest and Political Participation in the Ottoman Empire: Studies in Honor of Suraiya Faroqhi*, 127-142. İstanbul Bilgi Üniversitesi Yayınları.

Balla, E. and Johnson, N. D. (2009). Fiscal Crisis and Institutional Change in the Ottoman Empire and France. *The Journal of Economic History* 69(3), 809–845.

Bowles, S. (2004). *Microeconomics: Behavior, Institutions and Evolution*. Princeton University Press.

Coşgel, M. and Miceli, T. (2005). Risk, Transaction Costs, and Government Finance: The Distribution of Tax Revenue in the Ottoman Empire. *Journal of Economic History* 65(3), 806–21.

Coşgel, M. and Miceli, T. (2009). Tax Collection in History. *Public Finance Review* 37, 399–420.

Coşgel, M., Miceli, T. and Ahmad, R. (2009). Law, State Power and Taxation in Islamic History. *Journal of Economic Behavior and Organization* 71, 704–717.

Çizakça, M. (1993). Tax-Farming and Financial Decentralization in the Ottoman Empire, 1520-1697. *The Journal of European Economic History* 22, 219–250.

Çizakça, M. (1996). *Comparative Evolution of Business Partnerships: The Islamic World and Europe, with Special Reference to the Ottoman Archives*. Brill.

Darling, L. (1996). *Revenue-Rising and Legitimacy: Tax Collection and Finance Administration in the Ottoman Empire, 1560-1660*. Leiden: Brill.

Genç, M. (2000). *Osmanlı İmparatorluğu'nda Devlet ve Ekonomi*. Ötüken.

Greif, A. (1989). Reputation and Coalition in Medieval Trade: Evidence on the Maghribi Traders. *The Journal of Economic History* 49, 857–882.

Greif, A. (1993). Contract Enforceability and Economic Institutions in Early Trade: The Maghribi Traders' Coalition. *American Economic Review* 83(3), 525–548.

Greif, A. (2002). Economic History and Game Theory. In R. Aumann & S. Hart (Eds.), *Handbook of Game Theory with Economic Applications 3*, 1989–2024. North-Holland.

Hardin, G. (1968). The Tragedy of the Commons. *Science, New Series* 162(3859), 1243–1248.

İnalcık, H. (2000). *Osmanlı İmparatorluğu'nun Sosyal ve Ekonomik Tarihi I*. Eren.

İslamoğlu, H. and Keyder, Ç. (1977). Agenda for Ottoman History. *Review* 1, 31–55.

Johnson, N. D. and Koyama, M. (2017). States and Economic Growth: Capacity and Constraints. *Explorations in Economic History* 64, 1–20.

Karaman, K. (2009). Decentralized Coercion and Self-Restrain in Provincial Taxation: The Ottoman Empire 15th-16th Centuries. *Journal of Economic Behavior and Organization* 71, 690–703.

Karaman, K. and Pamuk, Ş. (2010). Ottoman State Finance in European Perspective, 1500–1914. *The Journal of Economic History* 70, 593–629.

Kennedy, P. (1988). *The Rise and Fall of the Great Powers*. Unwin Hyman.

Kiser, E. (1994). Markets and Hierarchies in Early Modern Tax Systems: A Principal-Agent Analysis. *Politics and Society*, 22, 284–315.

Kiser, E. (1999). Comparing Varieties of Agency Theory in Economics, Political Science, and Sociology: An Illustration from State Policy Implementation. *Sociological Theory* 17(2), 146–170.

Kuran, T. (2011). *The Long Divergence: How Islamic Law Held Back the Middle East*. Princeton University Press.

Ma, D. and Rubin, J. (2019). The Paradox of Power: Principal-Agent Problems and Administrative Capacity in Imperial China (and Other Absolutist Regimes). *Journal of Comparative Economics* 47, 277–294.
Monson, A. and Scheidel W. (Eds.) (2015). *Fiscal Regimes and the Political Economy of Premodern States*. Cambridge University Press.
North, D. (1991). Institutions. *The Journal of Economic Perspectives* 5(1), 97–112.
North, D. (1993). Institutions and Credible Commitment. *Journal of Institutional and Theoretical Economics (JITE) / Zeitschrift für die Gesamte* 149(1), 11–23.
North, D. and Weingast, B. (1989). Constitutions and Commitment: The Evolution of Institutions Governing Public Choice in Seventeenth-Century England. *The Journal of Economic History* 49, 803–832.
Ostrom, E. (1990). *Governing the Commons: The Evolution of Institutions for Collective Action*. Cambridge University Press.
Pamuk, Ş. (2004a). The Evolution of Financial Institutions in the Ottoman Empire, 1600–1914. *Financial History Review* 11, 7–32.
Pamuk, Ş. (2004b). Institutional Change and the Longevity of the Ottoman Empire, 1500–1800. *The Journal of Interdisciplinary History* 35, 225–247.
Pamuk, Ş. (2004c). Prices in the Ottoman Empire, 1469–1914. *International Journal of Middle East Studies* 36, 451–68.
Pomeranz, K. (2000). *The Great Divergence: China, Europe, and the Making of the Modern World Economy*. Princeton University Press.
Root, H. (1989). Tying the King's Hand: Credible Commitment and Royal Fiscal Policy during the Old Regime. *Rationality and Society* 1(2), 240–258.
Rubin, J. (2017). *Rules, Religion and Riches: Why the West Got Rich and the Middle East Did Not?* Cambridge University Press.
Salzmann, A. (1993). An Ancien Regime Revisited: "Privatization" and Political Economy in the Eighteenth-Century Ottoman Empire. *Politics and Society* 21, 393–423.
Salzmann, A. (2004). *Tocqueville in the Ottoman Empire: Rival Paths to the Modern State*. Brill.
Tilly, C. (1990). *Coercion, Capital and European States, AD 990-1992*. Basil Blackwell.
Van Zanden, J. L. (2009). *The Long Road to the Industrial Revolution: The European Economy in a Global Perspective, 1000–1800*. Brill.
Williamson, O. (1998). The Institutions of Governance. *The American Economic Review* 88(2), 75–79.

CHAPTER 10

Conclusion: Tax-Farming and Its Unintended Consequences

Fuat Oğuz

This book introduces a new methodology for understanding tax-farming contracts and the surrounding legal-economic relations in the Ottoman economic system. The Ottoman tax-farming system has long been a focal point in scholarly discourse on the fiscal and administrative strategies of the Ottoman Empire. Earlier studies have primarily examined tax-farming from the perspective of the state, viewing it as a tool for revenue collection and an administrative mechanism to meet the state's fiscal needs. However, this emphasis has often neglected the broader societal effects and the economic bargaining dynamics between the contracting parties. The evolution of tax-farming as an institution, shaped by unique Ottoman societal conditions and transactional issues, has frequently been overlooked.

F. Oğuz (✉)
Ankara, Türkiye
e-mail: foguz@yahoo.com

B. Altay (ed.), *Revenue-Raising Institutions, State Organization and Economic Change in the Early Modern Ottoman Empire*, Palgrave Studies in Economic History,
https://doi.org/10.1007/978-3-031-96492-3_10

Beginning with Bora Altay's outline of a new institutional model for understanding tax-farming in Chapter 3, this book reexamines the rise and fall of tax-farming from a fresh perspective. This concluding chapter revisits key discussions from previous chapters and highlights the institutional challenges surrounding tax-farming contracts.

Evolution of Tax-Farming and Unintended Consequences

The tax-farming system in the Ottoman Empire reflected the tensions between non-market allocation mechanisms and the market forces that shape the consequences of tax-farming contracts. The tax-farming model was not designed to maximize the product or transfer rent to the state. It was intended as a tool to finance military campaigns and administrative expenditures. The continuity of military expeditions was the overarching aim.

Tax-farming contracts emerged as responses to the prevailing institutional environment of the Ottoman Empire. The expansionist nature of the Empire put farming to a secondary place. Expeditions had to be financed and the transition to regular army required more resources. The inability of *Iltizam* to provide these sources forced the State to forego potential rents in the future to obtain larger sums at the beginning of the contract. The provision of lifetime contracts led to de facto decentralization as the state delegated authority in exchange for a larger lump-sum payment. The transition to the *malikane* system aimed to address the high transaction costs of administering the *Iltizam* system while reducing the uncertainty of short-term gains through long-term contracts.

The literature primarily examines the relationship between the State and its agents, particularly *mültezims* or tax-farmers. Given the archival basis of historical research, this focus is understandable. However, peasants who directly worked the land are often overlooked. From an economic standpoint, this omission poses a challenge to fully grasping the tax-farming system. Wealth was largely generated by third parties, such as peasants, who were not directly involved in tax-farming contracts.

The book begins with a conceptual discussion of the institution of tax-farming. Altay (Chapter 3) uses the principal-agent model to explore the relationship between the State and the tax-farmer. To some extent this is correct. The tax-farmer can be seen as an agent in terms of the function it plays. However, the institutional characteristics of tax-farming contracts brings tax-farming contracts closer to a market dealing. The owner of the land, the State, was interested in the rent. The tax-farmer acted as an independent contractor, or residual claimant. He made a profit or loss depending on his ability to collect revenue, the size of the harvest, and other conditions. Tax-farming contracts were not about the alignment of objectives of the State and tax-farmers. They were about providing revenue to the State from the land it owned. Since the tax amount was determined as a lump-sum payment at the auction, the State's intention to maximize the tax revenue ended with the auction. The collected revenue was not a tax in the modern sense. The state sold tax collecting rights to the highest bidder. It was rent based on State owned land. After all, the tax-farmer or the peasants did not own the land. The tax-farmer collected rent from peasants for the State. Even in the case of *Malikane*, the farmer could not bequeath his land to his children. There was no hereditary ownership and the land belonged to the Sultan.

The absolute power of the state created incentives for the Mültezim to manipulate the system, leading to a focus on short-term gains rather than long-term productivity. The lack of institutional mechanisms to reduce uncertainty and the state's ability to annul and resell contracts at will resulted in an inefficient system. The state's reluctance to establish a low-cost tax collection system, combined with high monitoring and information costs, initially made tax-farming viable. However, the state's opportunistic behavior, driven by increasing military and administrative expenditures, ultimately led to the system's collapse. The frequent annulment of contracts generated uncertainty, making tax-farming increasingly costly and unproductive. The state would annul the contract and resell it whenever it is expedient even in cases of lifetime contracting.

Over time, behavioral patterns institutionalized the state's opportunism, fostering demotivating beliefs among agents. As a result, tax-farming became a zero-sum game where profits were merely redistributed between the principal and the agent rather than fostering economic growth. Ramiz Üzümçeker's discussion in Chapter 5 highlights how the Sultan's absolute authority played a critical role in shaping tax-farming auctions and contracts. As widely discussed in earlier chapters, opportunistic behavior by the State lowered lump-sum payments as a result of high discount rates offered by potential tax-farmers. The lack of the credible commitments by the State and legal protections turned the relationship between the State and *Mültezim*s into a Prisoners' Dilemma game with cheating as the dominant strategy.

The Zero-Sum Logic of Ottoman Society and Tax-Farming Contracts

Islamic beliefs, particularly within the Sunni tradition, significantly influenced Ottoman society. The prevailing fatalistic and anti-materialistic worldview reinforced the notion of a "limited good," as described by George Foster (1962, 1965). Economic relations were perceived as a closed system, where one party's gain necessitated another's loss. Tax-farming contracts exemplified this logic, functioning as mechanisms for rent transfer from the agent to the principal. In this environment, both the State and the tax-farmers saw these contractual relations as zero-sum games where a predetermined surplus changed hands.

When there is a zero-sum component to economic interactions, demotivating beliefs emerge and spread, reducing incentives for productive effort and inhibiting economic development. The institution of tax-farming was a good example of zero-sum thinking.

The state's zero-sum perspective on tax-farming acted as a psychological tax on productive activity. The belief in resource scarcity encouraged rent-seeking behavior rather than entrepreneurial investment. The state did not view tax-farming as a means of generating wealth through trade or improving land productivity. Instead, it functioned primarily as a tool for wealth extraction to finance military and administrative expenditures.

In an agricultural society with minimal innovation, the absolutist state found tax-farming a convenient means of revenue extraction. Demotivating beliefs and unproductive entrepreneurship made tax-farming a viable yet ultimately detrimental option for the economy (see Üzümçeker, Chapter 5).

While there is now an extensive literature on *Iltizam* contracts, not much is written on the situation of farmers. As mentioned in earlier chapters, *mültezims* pressured farmers to maximize their revenues. This created an informal farming activity whenever possible. They did not have much incentive to improve observable products as the excess product would be captured by the agents. Instead, many farmers tried to change the contracted product to increase their output whenever it was difficult to observe their activities. *Mültezims* saw their relations with farmers as a zero-sum game. Since the production was limited, farmers' gains were their losses. Zero-sum thinking was at the root of the institution of *Iltizam*. Both the State and its agents believed that they had to share a predetermined sum of revenue. This way of thinking inhibited any gains from trade by both parties.

Discouragement of Profit-Seeking Entrepreneurship and Promotion of Rent-Seeking

The absolute power of the state over contracts, combined with the absence of legal protections for agents and farmers, transformed tax-farming into a rent-seeking rather than a profit-seeking activity. Uncertainty over contract duration discouraged investment in productivity. Having paid a substantial lump-sum to the state, agents prioritized short-term revenue extraction over sustainable development, knowing that the state could revoke their contracts at any time.

Both the *Iltizam* and *Malikane* systems prioritized rent extraction over productivity enhancement. The state aimed to minimize monitoring and information costs by assigning land for specific periods but left provinces largely autonomous in production matters. The lack of private property rights and the state's opportunism further discouraged investment, leading to unproductive entrepreneurship by both agents and the state.

In many cases, the state's behavior reduced land value and productive activity. The disparity between contracted and actual contract durations exemplifies how the state's policies inadvertently degraded land value. Agents, motivated by short-term profits, engaged in aggressive land exploitation, further diminishing its long-term worth. Uncertainty surrounding contracts led agents to allocate resources toward securing their contracts rather than improving productivity.

While the *malikane* system was introduced to encourage long-term investment and reduce tax collection uncertainty, it ultimately failed to achieve these goals. The inefficiencies of the auction mechanism increased transaction costs, compelling tax-farmers to hire local agents. This reliance on intermediaries highlighted the state's limited capacity to monitor tax collection effectively. The lack of secure property rights and persistent state opportunism reinforced rent-oriented behavior rather than productive investment.

The Ottoman state showed little interest in honoring the full duration of tax-farming contracts. Historical records indicate that actual contract durations were significantly shorter than their contracted terms (see Chapter 8). For example, as noted by Hande Nur Kırmızıkuşak and Özgür Hakan Aydoğmuş in Chapter 7, only 2 of 14 tax-farming contracts for Thessalonica customs were upheld between 1591 and 1619. Such breaches were widespread across the empire.

The absence of legal remedies for contract violations forced agents to rely on informal and personal relations with the state to protect their rights. As extensively discussed in the literature, tax-farming contracts exemplified the broader absence of the rule of law in the Ottoman Empire. The state strategically reauctioned contracts to extract more rent, creating an environment of perpetual uncertainty. Agents, recognizing these patterns, adapted their behavior accordingly, leading to lower revenue and increased opportunism on both sides.

In conclusion, the tax-farming system in the Ottoman Empire was characterized by inefficiency, rent-seeking, and uncertainty. The state's opportunistic behavior and lack of credible commitments undermined the potential benefits of tax-farming. Instead of fostering productive economic activity, the system incentivized short-term revenue extraction at the expense of long-term growth. The unintended consequence of these policies was the eventual decline of the tax-farming institution, as persistent uncertainty and opportunism rendered it unsustainable.

References

Foster, G. M. (1962). *Traditional Cultures, and the Impact of Technological Change*. Harper.

Foster, G. M. (1965). Peasant Society and the Image of Limited Good. *American Anthropologist* 67, 293–315.

Index

B. Altay (ed.), *Revenue-Raising Institutions, State Organization and Economic Change in the Early Modern Ottoman Empire*, Palgrave Studies in Economic History,
https://doi.org/10.1007/978-3-031-96492-3

GPSR Compliance

The European Union's (EU) General Product Safety Regulation (GPSR) is a set of rules that requires consumer products to be safe and our obligations to ensure this.

If you have any concerns about our products, you can contact us on ProductSafety@springernature.com

In case Publisher is established outside the EU, the EU authorized representative is:

Springer Nature Customer Service Center GmbH
Europaplatz 3
69115 Heidelberg, Germany

Batch number: 10755352

Printed by Printforce, the Netherlands